Kind Words

From Fellow Travelers

Before this primer went to print,
I shared the manuscript with a few friends –
ordinary people learning to abide.
Here's what they wanted you to know

***Franz**: "Charlie, I just finished reading the primer. My first impression is that this is your magnum opus – written by a man who understands what it means to abide. Every Christian should read this book. It reminds me of Miles J. Stanford's "The Complete Green Letters," but more accessible. I love the short, conversational tone. It's steeped in grace. I'm currently doing missionary work in Liberia. I plan to read one entry each morning with our teaching team before we go out to teach. The entries are short enough, but impactful enough to make us think all day. When the book is finished, I'll buy a box of copies to use with those I am discipling, to hold their hands through the process of learning to abide."*

Starla: *"I don't really have the words to tell you how deeply this is speaking to me. I feel these words in a very special and unique way – spiritual, as if we share a common bond. I'm on Day 17 and have cried all the way through it. Still crying now."* ***Starla,*** after her second reading: *"About five years ago, I spent the summer writing out my spiritual life story. I based it on the words 'abide in My love.' The word abide means so much to me. I remember my grandma praying John 15 all the time – 'Abide in Me and I in you.' When her life was at its* *hardest in her late 90s and her body would not function, she would sit in her chair or her bed, praying John 15 and Matthew 11:28. This devotional makes me feel like I felt with my grandma."*

John:[1] *"When I first opened this manuscript, I expected another book about trying harder to stay connected to Jesus. Instead, I found something rare: a primer that actually primes – a work that prepares the soul to receive what only God can give. Charlie writes in the tradition of Andrew Murray and Oswald Chambers, but with a warmth and accessibility all his own. It has the depth of those classic "abiding life" writers, without the density that can make them feel distant. He feels like a wise friend walking beside you – someone who doesn't just explain abiding but quietly creates space for it to happen. What struck me most is the tone. This book is deeply personal without being private; theologically rich without being academic; grace-centered without being soft on sin; repetitive without ever being boring. Somehow, reading it alone, you sense that you're part of a larger family learning the same rhythms of grace. The structure works beautifully – the three movements are intuitive: being loved (*Abide in Me*), being formed (*Christ in Me*), and being sent (*Jesus in Me, Living Through Me*). Each reflection feels just right – short enough to hold attention, deep enough to hold the heart. I found myself slowing down. Breathing differently. Not just reading about abiding but abiding as I read. The guides at the end are wise, offering practical handles without making the handles the point. This isn't just a book that informs the mind – it forms the soul. It's going to help people, deeply."*

---

[1] ***I would love to hear how this book lands with you as well. Feel free to write me at:***

abidinglifeprimer@gmail.com

THE ABIDING LIFE PRIMER

Jesus in Me,
Living Through Me,
For the Sake of Others

A 42-Day Devotional

by Charles F. Boyd

VINE & BRANCH PRESS

THE ABIDING LIFE PRIMER: *Jesus in Me, Living through Me, For the Sake of Others*

Abiding. adj. remaining, continuing, dwelling, living in close union with Christ so that His life flows through ours for the glory of God and the good of others.

Primer. n. a book that covers the basic elements of a subject. Pronounced "primm-er" (rhymes with "simmer.")

Cover design: Charles F. Boyd, adapted from a 100-year-old child's reading primer.

ISBN: 979-8-9954891-0-8

Printed in the United States of America

Vine & Branch Press, Greenville, SC
abidinglifeprimer@gmail.com

To my children and grandchildren:
my greatest joy and grateful legacy.
May you know, more than anything else,
what it means to abide in Christ.

Introduction

This primer is a simple daily tool to help believers experience more fully the abiding life of Christ—Jesus living in us, through us, and for the sake of others. Like a child's primer that teaches the basics of reading, this book invites Christians to rehearse day by day the foundational reality of union with Christ: "Christ in me, the hope of glory" (Colossians 1:27), learning to rest in His indwelling life rather than striving in our own strength.

Many years ago, I was given a small book titled *A Gospel Primer for Christians* by Milton Vincent. That little primer has had a profound, Gospel-clarifying impact on thousands of Christ-followers—and especially on me. Day after day, Milton's short, personal reflections and Scripture passages helped me preach the Gospel to myself, reminding me that my acceptance before God rests entirely on Christ's finished work. It freed me from the treadmill of performance and re-centered my heart on grace. I am deeply grateful for it; it remains one of the most helpful resources I've ever used, and I still return to it regularly to preach the Gospel to myself.

The Abiding Life Primer is not meant to replace Milton's book, but to build on the same kind of daily rehearsal habit he modeled so well. Where *A Gospel Primer* keeps the Gospel front and center in our identity and justification, this primer turns that same gaze toward the ongoing reality of Christ's indwelling presence—the "double incarnation": Christ with us in his first coming, and Christ within us now by his Spirit.

The New Testament repeatedly calls us not only to believe the Gospel but to abide in Christ so that His life flows through ours (John 15:4–5; Galatians 2:20). Yet we so easily forget this union amid daily pressures, temptations, and self-effort. This book is an invitation to preach this abiding truth to yourself daily, letting it reshape your heart, relationships, and ordinary moments.

You will notice that certain themes and Scriptures appear more than once. That is intentional. A primer works by gentle repetition—circling back over the same truth from slightly different angles—so that, over time, those truths sink below the level of mere information and begin to renew the way we think, pray, and live. My hope is that the repeated language and passages will become familiar friends the Spirit uses to retrain your reflexes toward grace and dependence on Christ.

How to use this primer

There are 42 reflections, grouped into three movements that build on one another. Reflections 1–14—*Abide in Me and I in You*—explore our ache for home, God making His home in us, and how He invites us to abide in Jesus, in His love, and in His word.

Reflections 15–28— *I am in Christ and Christ is in me* —unpack how the apostle Paul gives language to the abiding life in what this primer calls the "double incarnation," then move to Paul's incredible statement, "It is no longer I who live, but Christ lives in me," and on to the grace-driven process by which the Spirit forms Jesus' life in us.

Finally, Reflections 29–42—*Jesus in Me, Living Through Me, For the Sake of Others* show how Christ's indwelling presence meets us in ordinary days, in our shared life as His body, in trials and pruning, and in His ongoing mission until we are finally home with Him.

You might try reading one entry per day, following a simple 6-week, 7-day plan or a

7-week, 6-day plan. Consider getting a simple journal where you can jot down thoughts, questions, and insights that surface as you walk through each day's reading. I have found that writing helps me notice what the Spirit is surfacing in my mind and heart and gives me a way to look back and trace His faithful work over time.

Begin by reading the day's reflection, letting it speak personally to your soul, and jot down in your journal any words or phrases that the Holy Spirit may highlight for you. Then turn the reflection into prayer—for example, if a line reads, "I am already known, loved, and secure as the Father's child" (Day 11), you might pray, "Lord, help me live today from this truth—to rest in being known by You, to receive Your love, and to find my security in You alone."

You'll also notice that in each reflection, one line appears in **bold**. This is not because it is the most important line, but because it can serve as a suggested "prayer prompt"—an on-ramp to help you talk to God about what you just read. For example, if the bold line is, "In His hands, even losses, delays, and disappointments become sacred tools for forming me into the image of Christ," you might pray:

"Jesus, teach me to bring my grief to You. When I don't understand Your ways, help me stay near enough to trust You with everything. Yes, Lord, use what I'm going through to make me more like You." This small practice turns reflection into communion. Of course, the Holy Spirit may highlight other words, phrases, or sentences that can help you turn these reflections from simply being "something you read" into "something you pray" and that can move you from information to formation.

After you have prayed, read the Scripture passages slowly, asking the Holy Spirit to take God's Word in the text and make it God's word to you personally. Underline or circle words and phrases in the passages that connect back to the reflection so that the link between the text and the reflection becomes clear in your mind and heart.

And then carry the truth from the reflection and the Scripture passages that the Holy Spirit has impressed on you with you through the day—perhaps repeating the simple daily confession from reflection 37: "Jesus, You live in me; live Your life through me today, for the sake of others."

At the end, you'll find a list of "One Sentence Summaries" of each of the 42 reflections. You can use these as a final review day, between sections as a refresher, or any time you need a brief "big-picture" realignment with the heart of the abiding life. In fact, you might find it helpful to read these at the beginning to get a 30,000-foot flyover so you have a sense of the journey you are beginning. You may want to underline or note the statements that especially speak to you or copy one or two into your journal as a specific prayer or confession for the coming week.

When you finish the daily reflections, don't stop there. The final section, *Practicing the Abiding Life,* offers five simple guides that show what this can look like in real life—in your schedule, your thought life, your work, your relationships, and even your experience of joy. Think of them as on-ramps into living what you've just been praying and pondering.

A brief word about language. These reflections use the singular "I" and "me" voice because abiding is deeply personal and each of us must learn to trust Jesus in the concrete details of our own lives. This parallels how Paul talked about his life in Christ in Galatians

2:20—"I have been crucified with Christ. It is no longer I who live but Christ lives in me." Yet in the New Testament, teaching about abiding and the Spirit's work most often speaks in the plural "you"—a people, a body, a temple—what some have called the "y'all" of life in Christ. As you walk through these reflections, remember that "Christ in me" is always part of "Christ in us," and that the ultimate outworking of "Jesus living in me, to live His life through me" is always "for the *sake* of others," and with the *help* of others.

My prayer is that this primer will help you abide more consciously in Christ, experience His life flowing through your ordinary days, and overflow in love for others—all to the glory of the Father, Son, and Holy Spirit.

Grace and peace to you in the abiding life of Jesus.

Charlie Boyd

Greenville, South Carolina
2026

Table of Contents

II. *I am in Christ and Christ is in me* (15-28)

Day 15	The first incarnation – Christ with me and for me
Day 16	The second incarnation – Christ in me, forming His life in me
Day 17	The normal Christian life
Day 18	From outside-in religion to inside-out life
Day 19	My old self crucified with Christ
Day 20	I no longer live the life I live
Day 21	Walking by the Spirit = Jesus living through me
Day 22	Rescued from this present evil age
Day 23	Free from guilt and the treadmill of performance
Day 24	Grace as the engine of change
Day 25	Christ being formed in me
Day 26	Spiritual formation as the Spirit's work
Day 27	Free to love, not to indulge
Day 28	Love fulfilling the law through me

III. *Jesus in Me, Living through Me, For the Sake of Others* (29-42)

Day 29	The fruit of the Spirit is the abiding life made visible
Day 30	Jesus living through me in my relationships
Day 31	Jesus living through me in failure and weakness
Day 32	Jesus living through me in opportunity and risk
Day 33	Jesus living through me in the mundane and monotonous
Day 34	From God-amnesia to God-awareness
Day 35	Silent prayer as resting in the One who lives in me
Day 36	Slow, Spirit-guided Scripture Reading as abiding in His word
Day 37	My daily confession
Day 38	Saying "no" to moral reformation, "yes" to Gospel transformation
Day 39	Seeing trials and pruning as the Father's wise love
Day 40	Abiding together: Christ in us as His body

Part I

(days 1-14)

Abide in Me and I in You

God makes His home in me through Christ and invites me to abide in Him – receiving His pruning, depending on His life, letting His words abide in Me, and walking in His love – so that Jesus' own character and joy grow in me and flow through me.

1. My deep ache for home

There is a quiet ache that lives in my heart, a longing I can't quite name, that surfaces in my loneliest and most honest moments. Sometimes it feels like homesickness for a place I remember, and sometimes like a yearning for a home I've never yet known. Even when life goes well, I sense that I am not yet fully "there," that something in me still waits and watches for a "better country." The Scriptures tell me this ache is not strange but normal for the people of God, who have always confessed themselves to be strangers and exiles on the earth, seeking a heavenly homeland. My restlessness, then, is not psychological; it is spiritual, a built-in homing device that keeps me from mistaking any earthly house for my true home. **This abiding ache is actually a gift. It keeps me searching—beyond my own comfort, careers, and compulsions—toward the One in whom my soul was made to dwell.**

Hebrews 11:13-16 — These all died in faith, not having received the things promised, but having seen them and greeted them from afar, and having acknowledged that they were strangers and exiles on the earth. For people who speak thus make it clear that they are seeking a homeland. If they had been thinking of that land from which they had gone out, they would have had opportunity to return. But as it is, they desire a better country, that is, a heavenly one. Therefore, God is not ashamed to be called their God, for he has prepared for them a city. **Psalm 84:1-2** – How lovely is your dwelling place, O LORD of hosts! My soul longs, yes, faints for the courts of the LORD; my heart and flesh sing for joy to the living God. **2 Corinthians 5:1-8** – For we know that if the tent that is our earthly home is destroyed, we have a building from God, a house not made with hands, eternal in the heavens. For in this tent we groan, longing to put on our heavenly dwelling, if indeed by putting it on we may not be found naked. For while we are still in this tent, we groan, being burdened—not that we would be unclothed, but that we would be further clothed, so that what is mortal may be swallowed up by life. He who has prepared us for this very thing is God, who has given us the Spirit as a guarantee. So, we are always of good courage. We know that while we are at home in the body, we are away from the Lord, for we walk by faith, not by sight. Yes, we are of good courage, and we would rather be away from the body and at home with the Lord. **Philippians 3:20** – But our citizenship is in heaven, and from it we await a Savior, the Lord Jesus Christ.

2. God has made His home in my heart

Into this ache for home, Jesus speaks a staggering promise: "In that day you will know that I am in My Father, and you in Me, and I in you." When I trusted Christ, the Father, Son, and Holy Spirit came not only to be *with* me but to live *in* me, making my heart Their home. I am no longer merely a wanderer longing for God; I am a dwelling place in which God Himself delights to reside. This means my truest "address" is no longer a street or city, but me in Christ and Christ in me. The One who holds all things together has chosen to take up residence in my innermost being, not as an occasional visitor but as a permanent, loving Presence. When I forget this, I live like a spiritual orphan; **when I remember it, I discover that the home my heart has always longed for has already begun inside of me**.

John 14:18–23 – "I will not leave you as orphans; I will come to you. Yet a little while and the world will see me no more, but you will see me. Because I live, you also will live. In that day you will know that I am in my Father, and you in me, and I in you. Whoever has my commandments and keeps them, he it is who loves me. And he who loves me will be loved by my Father, and I will love him and manifest myself to him." Judas (not Iscariot) said to him, "Lord, how is it that you will manifest yourself to us, and not to the world?" Jesus answered him, "If anyone loves me, he will keep my word, and my Father will love him, and we will come to him and make our home with him."
Colossians 1:26–27 – [This is] the mystery

hidden for ages and generations but now revealed to his saints. To them God chose to make known how great among the Gentiles are the riches of the glory of this mystery, which is Christ in you, the hope of glory. **Romans 8:9-11** – You, however, are not in the flesh but in the Spirit, if in fact the Spirit of God dwells in you. Anyone who does not have the Spirit of Christ does not belong to him. But if Christ is in you, although the body is dead because of sin, the Spirit is life because of righteousness. If the Spirit of him who raised Jesus from the dead dwells in you, he who raised Christ Jesus from the dead will also give life to your mortal bodies through his Spirit who dwells in you. **Galatians 4:6** – And because you are sons, God has sent the Spirit of his Son into our hearts, crying, "Abba! Father!"

3. Abide in Me as I abide in You

Because God has made His home in me, Jesus now invites me to make my home in Him: "Abide in Me, and I in you." Abiding is more than merely staying connected; it is learning to live from the place where He and I already share life together. To abide is to turn again and again from simply living in my head to dropping down into the inner room of my heart where Christ and I are quietly present to one another. It is the Spirit who makes this inner room real to me, awakening my awareness of Jesus' presence—both with me and within me. Abiding is not something reserved for a few, graduate-level believers; it is the normal Christian life Jesus describes in John 15 – His life in me and my life in Him. Each day I choose whether to move through life as if Jesus were far away, or to receive His invitation to live in conscious, trusting fellowship with the One who already lives in me. **When I abide, I am not trying to get Him to come near; I am waking up to the reality that He has already chosen to remain near, within me**.

John 14:20 – In that day you will know that I am in my Father, and you in me, and I in you. **John 14:23** – Jesus answered him, "If anyone loves me, he will keep my word, and my Father will love him, and we will come to him and make our home with him." **John 15:4–5** – Abide in me, and I in you. As the branch cannot bear fruit by itself, unless it abides in the vine, neither can you, unless you abide in me. I am the vine; you are the branches. Whoever abides in me and I in him, he it is that bears much fruit, for apart from me you can do nothing. **Galatians 2:20** – I have been crucified with Christ. It is no longer I who live, but Christ who lives in me. And the life I now live in the flesh I live by faith in the Son of God, who loved me and gave himself for me. **Romans 8:10–11** – But if Christ is in you, although the body is dead because of sin, the Spirit is life because of righteousness. If the Spirit of him who raised Jesus from the dead dwells in you, he who raised Christ Jesus from the dead will also give life to your mortal bodies through his Spirit who dwells in you.

4. Jesus the true Vine, I the branch

Jesus calls Himself the True Vine and names me as one of His branches. Just as a branch has no independent life, so I was never designed to live the Christian life by my own strength or religious willpower. My whole calling is to remain where I already am—joined to Him by grace—so that His very life can flow freely through me. Every attempt to live *for* Jesus without living *from* Jesus leaves me dry, anxious, and fruitless, like a cut branch slowly withering on the ground. But when I own my "branch-ness," confess my "apart-from-Him-I-can-do-nothing-ness," and relax the weight of my soul onto the Vine, His strength begins to do in me and through me what I could never do for myself. **The Christian life, then, is not me straining to imitate Christ from the outside-in, but Christ imparting His life to me from the inside-out**, just as a vine shares its life with the branch.

John 15:4–5 — Abide in me, and I in you. As the branch cannot bear fruit by itself, unless it abides in the vine, neither can you, unless you abide in me. I am the vine; you are the branches. Whoever abides in me and I in him, he it is that bears much fruit, for apart from me you can do nothing. **2 Corinthians 3:5** – Not that we are sufficient in ourselves to claim anything as coming from us, but our sufficiency is from God. **Philippians 4:13** I can do all things through him who strengthens me.

5. The Father, my wise Vinedresser

If Jesus is the Vine and I am a branch, then my Father is the wise and loving Vinedresser who cares for every branch in the whole vineyard. He watches my life not with detached criticism but with a gardener's eye, always seeking what will bring about the richest and most lasting fruit. When He prunes me, cutting back comforts, illusions, or even good things, He is not punishing me but making room for more of His Son's life to show through. Because of the Gospel, I do not have to fear the Vinedresser's shears; the same Father who did not spare His own Son will never prune me needlessly. **In His hands, even losses, delays, and disappointments become sacred tools for forming me into the image of Christ**. As I learn to trust His pruning, I can begin to welcome His wise interruptions, knowing that He is far more committed to my fruitfulness than I am.

John 15:1-2 – I am the true vine, and my Father is the vinedresser. Every branch in me that does not bear fruit he takes away, and every branch that does bear fruit he prunes, that it may bear more fruit. **Hebrews 12:5-11** – And have you forgotten the exhortation that addresses you as sons? "My son do not regard lightly the discipline of the Lord, nor be weary when reproved by him. For the Lord disciplines the one he loves and chastises every son whom he receives." It is for discipline that you have to endure. God is treating you as sons. For what son is there whom his father does not discipline? If you are left without discipline, in which all have participated, then you are illegitimate children and not sons. Besides this, we have had earthly fathers who disciplined us and we respected them. Shall we not much more be subject to the Father of spirits and live? For they disciplined us for a short time as it seemed best to them, but he disciplines us for our good, that we may share his holiness. For the moment all discipline seems painful rather than pleasant, but later it yields the peaceful fruit of righteousness to those who have been trained by it. **Romans 8:28-29** – And we know that for those who love God all things work together for good, for those who are called according to his purpose. For those whom he foreknew he also predestined to be conformed to the image of his Son, in order that he might be the firstborn among many brothers. **James 1:2-4** – Count it all joy, my brothers, when you meet trials of various kinds, for you know that the testing of your faith produces steadfastness. And let steadfastness have its full effect, that you may be perfect and complete, lacking in nothing.

6. Already pruned by His Word

Jesus says I am already "clean"—already "pruned" (*same Greek word*)—because of the Word He has spoken to me. His Gospel Word cut me away from my old ways of trying to save myself and grafted me into the True Vine by sheer grace. Before the Father ever lifts a pruning knife in my circumstances, He has already done a decisive, once-for-all pruning in my identity. This means I do not live the abiding life to become acceptable; I abide because I have already been cleansed and welcomed in Christ. Every command of Jesus now comes to me, not as condemnation from a Judge, but as guidance from the Gardener who has already claimed me as His own. **Remembering that I am already pruned by His word frees me to receive further pruning without fear**—trusting that the Father's cuts, though sometimes sharp, always follow the decisive cleansing of the Gospel.

John 15:2–3 – Every branch in me that does not bear fruit he takes away, and every branch that does bear fruit he prunes, that it may bear more fruit. Already you are clean because of the word that I have spoken to you. **John 13:10** – Jesus said to him, "The one who has bathed does not need to wash, except for his feet, but is completely clean. And you are clean, but not every one of you." **Titus 3:4–7** – But when the goodness and loving kindness of God our Savior appeared, he saved us, not because of works done by us in righteousness, but according to his own mercy, by the washing of regeneration and renewal of the Holy Spirit, whom he poured out on us richly through Jesus Christ our Savior, so that being justified by his grace we might become heirs according to the hope of eternal life.

7. Pruned again for even more fruit

Though "already" pruned, the Father continues to prune every branch that does bear fruit so that it will bear even more. In love, He removes what is merely leafy busyness, outward success, or self-reliant ministry so that the life of Jesus can run more freely through me. Pruning seasons often feel like loss, confusion, or limitation, yet they are actually the Father's way of protecting me from the self-directed story I keep trying to write and preparing me for deeper fruitfulness. When my plans are cut back, my illusions of control are being cut back with them. The Father is not trying to make my life smaller; He is making space for a larger love, a quieter joy, and a more Spirit-formed character to ripen in me. **If I can learn to see my disappointments**

through the eye of the Vinedresser, I may begin to thank Him not only for what He gives but even for what He takes away. In all of this, the fruit does not earn me God's favor; it grows out of the favor He has already placed over me in Jesus. It is the gracious evidence that I already belong to Him in Christ.

John 15:2 —Every branch in me that does not bear fruit he takes away, and every branch that does bear fruit he prunes, that it may bear more fruit. **Hebrews 12:5–11** — And have you forgotten the exhortation that addresses you as sons? "My son do not regard lightly the discipline of the Lord, nor be weary when reproved by him. For the Lord disciplines the one he loves and chastises every son whom he receives." It is for discipline that you have to endure. God is treating you as sons. For what son is there whom his father does not discipline? If you are left without discipline, in which all have participated, then you are illegitimate children and not sons. Besides this, we have had earthly fathers who disciplined us and we respected them. Shall we not much more be subject to the Father of spirits and live? For they disciplined us for a short time as it seemed best to them, but he disciplines us for our good, that we may share his holiness. For the moment all discipline seems painful rather than pleasant, but later it yields the peaceful fruit of righteousness to those who have been trained by it. **James 1:2–4** Count it all joy, my brothers, when you meet trials of various kinds, for you know that the testing of your faith produces steadfastness. And let steadfastness have its full effect, that you may be perfect and complete, lacking in nothing. **Romans 8:28–29** – And we know that for those who love God all things work together for good, for those who are called according to his purpose. For those whom he foreknew he also predestined to be conformed to the image of his Son, in order that he might be the firstborn among many brothers. **1 Thessalonians 5:18** –Give thanks in all circumstances; for this is the will of God in Christ for you.

8. The life of the Vine flowing through me

Abiding means that the life of the Vine—Jesus Himself—flows into and through me as naturally as sap runs through a living branch. His compassion, mercy, purity, and strength are not distant ideals; they are present resources, available moment by moment in the indwelling Christ. **Whatever good fruit appears in my life is not the result of my willpower, but the expression of His life, quietly at work in my inner being**—a gift that shows I am His, not a payment that makes me His. As I enjoy nearness to Him in Word and prayer, His desires begin to reshape my desires, His thoughts begin to retrain my thoughts, and His love begins to soften my reactions. The same Jesus who walked through Galilee now walks through my day, meeting people and situations through my words, my hands, and my presence. And as His life flows into me, it is also flowing through every other branch attached to the Vine. I am one branch among many, and the sap that sustains me is the same sap that sustains my brothers and sisters in Christ. Their fruitfulness and mine are bound together in the one Vine. The abiding life is nothing less than the incarnate Christ continuing to live His life in and through me, and together, through us.

John 15:5 —I am the vine; you are the branches. Whoever abides in me and I in him, he it is that bears much fruit, for apart from me you can do nothing. **John 15:8** — By this my Father is glorified, that you bear much fruit and so prove to be my disciples. **Galatians 2:20** — I have been crucified with Christ. It is no longer I who live, but Christ who lives in me. And the life I now live in the flesh I live by faith in the Son of God, who loved me and gave himself for me. **Colossians 1:27–28** —To them God chose to make known how great among the Gentiles are the riches of the glory of this mystery, which is Christ in you, the hope of glory. Him we proclaim, warning everyone and teaching everyone with all wisdom, that we may present everyone mature in Christ. For this I toil, struggling with all his energy that he powerfully works within me. **Romans 8:10–11** — But if Christ is in you, although the body is dead because of sin, the Spirit is life because of righteousness. If the Spirit of him who raised Jesus from the dead dwells in you, he who raised Christ Jesus from the dead will also give life to your mortal bodies through his Spirit who dwells in you.

9. Fruit as Jesus' own character in me

The fruit the Father seeks is not impressiveness, but likeness—the character of Jesus reproduced in me by the Spirit. Love, joy, peace, patience, kindness, goodness, faithfulness, gentleness, and self-control are not nine separate virtues we strive to attain; they are nine facets of one life, the life of Christ in me. As this fruit ripens, people do not walk away impressed with my discipline or resolve; they walk away having tasted something of Jesus. And this kind of fruit cannot be microwaved or manufactured; it grows slowly as I live from my new identity in Christ rather than from my performance-driven flesh. Change is not the condition of my acceptance, but the consequence of having been accepted in Christ. **Rules can restrain my behavior for a while, but only the indwelling Spirit can reshape my heart into the image of the Son**.

And as He does, He is not erasing who I am but redeeming it. In friendship with Jesus, I am becoming the particular son or daughter the Father has always desired, a real person whose unique story and temperament now serve the revelation of Christ in the world around me. The abiding life lifts my eyes from "Am I doing enough?" to "Is Jesus' life in me becoming more visible in how I think, feel, choose, and in how I love others in the body of Christ?" In this way, our shared life together becomes the vineyard where the world tastes and sees His love. (*see page 124 for more on "fruit-bearing"*)

John 15:8 —By this my Father is glorified, that you bear much fruit and so prove to be my disciples. **Galatians 5:16–23**— But I say, walk by the Spirit, and you will not gratify the desires of the flesh. For the desires of the flesh are against the Spirit, and the desires of the Spirit are against the flesh, for these are opposed to each other, to keep you from doing the things you want to do. But if you are led by the Spirit, you are not under the law. Now the works of the flesh are evident: sexual immorality, impurity, sensuality, idolatry, sorcery, enmity, strife, jealousy, fits of anger, rivalries, dissensions, divisions, envy, drunkenness, orgies, and things like these. I warn you, as I warned you before, that those who do such things will not inherit the kingdom of God. But the fruit of the Spirit is love, joy, peace, patience, kindness, goodness, faithfulness, gentleness, self-control; against such things there is no law. **Romans 8:29** — For those whom he foreknew he also predestined to be conformed to the image of his Son, in order that he might be the firstborn among many brothers. **2 Corinthians 3:18** — And we all, with unveiled face, beholding the glory of the Lord, are being transformed into the same image from one degree of glory to another. For this comes from the Lord who is the Spirit.

10. Apart from Him I can do nothing

Jesus' words, "Apart from Me you can do nothing," expose the illusion that I can live the Christian life by managing my own religious performance. I might accomplish many impressive things in my own strength, but in heaven's accounting, anything not sourced in the Vine amounts to nothing of eternal weight. This is not meant to shame me; it is an invitation to freedom from the exhausting burden of self-salvation and self-transformation. When I embrace my dependence instead of resisting it, I become most fruitful in the very places where I feel weakest. The same grace that saved me apart from works is the grace that now bears fruit in me apart from self-reliance. In this way, fruit is the outflow of grace already given, not a benchmark I must reach to keep God pleased with me. **To confess, "Lord, apart from You, I can do nothing," is not resignation; it is a doorway into the life where Christ in me can do far more than all I ask or imagine.**

John 15:5 – I am the vine; you are the branches. Whoever abides in me and I in him, he it is that bears much fruit, for apart from me you can do nothing. **2 Corinthians 3:5** – Not that we are sufficient in ourselves to claim anything as coming from us, but our sufficiency is from God. **Ephesians 3:21** – Now to him who is able to do far more abundantly than all that we ask or think, according to the power at work within us, to him be glory in the church and in Christ Jesus throughout all generations, forever and ever. Amen. **Philippians 2:12–13** – Therefore, my beloved, as you have always obeyed, so now, not only as in my presence but much more in my absence, work out your own salvation with fear and trembling, for it is God who works in you, both to will and to work for his good pleasure.

11. Abide in My Word

The moment I trust Christ, I am set free from rule-based religion and the guilt of falling short. But all too often, there's a gap between the freedom that is already mine in Christ and my daily experience. Jesus calls me to let His word abide in me, not as religious ideals but as His living voice. He promises that abiding in His word brings a freedom I can experience—freedom from the ingrained patterns of the flesh that once held me captive. When I pay attention, I can name where I am not experiencing the freedom Jesus died to give me: the pull to perform, the need to look good, the mental loops I run, and how I try to manage outcomes. In those moments, I may say I believe Him, but I am not taking Him at His word. His word tells me I am already known, loved, and secure as the Father's child. To abide is to keep returning my thoughts to what He has said until His truth—not my anxieties or others' opinions—becomes my natural way of thinking. This is not abstract. In conflict, I remember how Jesus entrusted Himself to the Father. When anxiety rises, I remember the Father knows what I need. When I lean on my own understanding, I choose to trust what He has spoken. **If I do not take my thoughts captive to His word, they will take me captive**. Over time, as His word dwells in me, my mind is renewed. Abiding in His word is not an added burden but the way His truth and freedom quietly take root within me. *(See page 109 to dig deeper into abiding in Jesus' word.)*

Galatians 5:1 – [It was] for freedom [that] Christ has set us free; stand firm, therefore, and do not submit again to a yoke of slavery. **John 8:31–32** – So Jesus said to the Jews who had believed him, "If you abide in my word, you are truly my disciples, and you will know the truth, and the truth will set you free." **John 15:7** – "If you abide in me, and my words abide in you, ask whatever you wish, and it will be done for you." **John 17:17** "Sanctify them in the truth; your word is truth." **Psalm 1:1–3** – Blessed is the man who walks not in the counsel of the wicked... but his delight is in the law of the LORD, and on his law, he meditates day and night. He is like a tree planted by streams of water.

12. Abide in My love

When Jesus says, "As the Father has loved me, so have I loved you. Abide in My love," He is not putting me on probation or asking me to earn what He has already freely given. **I do not obey in order to be loved; I am loved, and therefore I obey**. His commands show me how to remain within, and experience, the circle of His love—how to walk in step with the One who has my deepest good at heart. Because the One who commands me also lives within me by His Spirit, obedience is no longer a self-powered project but a sharing in His own patience, courage, and holiness as I yield to Him. When I disobey, I do not stop being loved, but I step outside the enjoyment of that love and feel again the misery of trying to run my life on my own. My obedience, then, does not earn His love; it simply positions me to enjoy the love that is already mine in Christ. And this love, once received, is never meant to stop with me. The law once condemned me; now, in Christ, His commands become love's pathways, keeping me close to the heart of the One who has pledged to never let me go.

John 15:9–10 – As the Father has loved me, so have I loved you. Abide in my love. If you keep my commandments, you will abide in my love, just as I have kept my Father's commandments and abide in his love. **John 14:15** – If you love me, you will keep my commandments. **John 14:21** – Whoever has my commandments and keeps them, he it is who loves me ... **John 14:23** – Jesus answered him, If anyone loves me, he will keep my word, and my Father will love him, and we will come to him and make our home with him. **John 13:34–35** – A new command I give you: Love one another. As I have loved you, so you must love one another. By this everyone will know that you are my disciples, if you love one another. **Titus 2:11–12** – For the grace of God has appeared ... training us to renounce ungodliness... and to live self-controlled, upright, and godly lives in the present age. **Romans 6:14** – For sin will have no dominion over you, since you are not under law but under grace.

13. Obedience as abiding in His love

When Jesus links love and obedience, He is inviting me into a life where obedience is the lived expression of love, not a way to buy His favor. Obedience is not a cold duty performed for a distant Master; it is the practical shape of trusting the One who has given Himself for me. As I keep His word, I stay within the experience of His love—like remaining within the warmth of a fire rather than wandering into the cold. When I resist His commands, I am not merely breaking a rule; I am stepping away from the One who loves me most. Abiding in His love means increasingly learning to say "Yes" to His voice, even when I do not fully understand, believing that His heart is better for me than my own plans. In this way, **obedience becomes less about willpower and more about relationship: listening to Jesus, trusting His wisdom, and walking with Him in the paths where His love is most deeply known**. And this obedience is never merely private. Jesus Himself said, "A new command I give you: Love one another. As I have loved you, so you must love one another. By this everyone will know that you are my disciples, if you love one another". The love I receive while abiding in Him is the very love I am called to extend. Obedience to His command to love others is not an add-on to the abiding life; it is the abiding life made visible in community. When I love a brother or sister—forgiving, serving, bearing with them—I am not merely being "nice"; I am demonstrating that Christ's love actually lives in me. My obedience becomes a signpost pointing others to the One whose love I am learning to trust.

John 15:9–10 – As the Father has loved me, so have I loved you. Abide in my love. If you keep my commandments, you will abide in my love…. **John 14:21** – Whoever has my commandments and keeps them, he it is who loves me … **John 14:23** – If anyone loves me, he will keep my word, and my Father will love him, and we will come to him and make our home with him. **Titus 2:11–12** – For the grace of God has appeared … training us to renounce ungodliness… and to live self-controlled, upright, and godly lives in the present age. **Romans 6:14** – For sin will have no dominion over you, since you are not under law but under grace. **John 13:34–35** – A new command I give you: Love one another. As I have loved you, so you must love one another. By this everyone will know that you are my disciples, if you love one another.

14. Homesick for heaven, at home in Him now

The more I taste of Christ's love, the more my heart longs for the day when I will see Him face to face in the home He is preparing for me. Like the saints of old, I confess that I am a stranger and exile on the earth, seeking a better country, a heavenly one. Yet I do not wait for heaven as if God were far away; the One who will one day welcome me into His house has already made His home in my heart. My present abiding in Him is a foretaste of my future dwelling with Him, and every glimpse of His presence now is a down payment on the day when homesickness will be forever healed in the fullness of His glory. But this future hope shapes my present relationships. Because I am destined for a kingdom where love reigns perfectly, I am freed to love imperfect people now without demanding that they satisfy me. My ultimate home is not with them but with Him—and that means I can serve them, forgive them, and bear with them without expecting them to be my heaven. **The abiding life "for the sake of others" means that the love I receive from Christ flows through me toward my brothers and sisters**, and together we become a pilgrim people, learning to love one another as we journey toward our final home. In this way, our shared life now becomes a foretaste of the perfect communion that awaits us when we are finally home with Him.

Hebrews 11:13–16 — These all died in faith, not having received the things promised, but having seen them and greeted them from afar, and having acknowledged that they were strangers and exiles on the earth. For people who speak thus make it clear that they are seeking a homeland. If they had been thinking of that land from which they had gone out, they would have had opportunity to return. But as it is, they desire a better country, that is, a heavenly one. Therefore, God is not ashamed to be called their God, for he has prepared for them a city. **John 14:2–3** – In my Father's house are many rooms. If it were not so, would I have told you that I go to prepare a place for you? And if I go and prepare a place for you, I will come again and will take you to myself, that where I am you may be also. **John 14:23** –Jesus answered him, "If anyone loves me, he will keep my word, and my Father will love him, and we will come to him and make our home with him." **Philippians 3:20–21** – But our citizenship is in heaven, and from it we await a Savior, the Lord Jesus Christ, who will transform our lowly body to be like his glorious body, by the power that enables him even to subject all things to himself. **1John 4:11–12** – Dear friends, since God so loved us, we also ought to love one another. No one has ever seen God; but if we love one another, God lives in us and his love is made complete in us.

Thoughts & Observations

Part II

(Days 15-28)

I Am in Christ and Christ is In Me

In the "double incarnation," the Christ who once came for me to be with me now lives in me by His Spirit, freeing me from the condemnation of rule-based religion and gradually forming His own life in me as the true engine of life-change – not my own striving.

15. The first incarnation: Christ with me and for me

Jesus' teaching on abiding finds its deep theological echo in Paul's language of being "in Christ" and Christ "in us"—but it all begins here, in what this Primer calls the "double incarnation"—**God incarnated Himself in Jesus so Jesus could be incarnated in me**. In the first incarnation, in what the apostle Paul calls a "great mystery," the eternal Son took on human flesh and became "Immanuel, God with us" (Isaiah 7:14; Matthew 1:23). He entered our broken world to reveal the Father's heart, to live a sinless life as the true Son of Abraham, and to fulfill all righteousness on my behalf. He bore the curse of the law my sins deserved, died in my place, rose again, and reconciled me to the Father. He came to be *with* me and *for* me—His perfect life, atoning death, and victorious resurrection securing my standing with God entirely apart from anything I have done or failed to do. Whenever I doubt God's heart toward me, I look again to the incarnate, crucified, risen Jesus and remember that His finished work is the unshakeable foundation of my acceptance.

1 Timothy 3:16 —Without question, this is the *great mystery* of our faith: Christ was revealed in a human body ..." (*my paraphrase*) **Galatians 4:4-6** — But when the fullness of time had come, God sent forth his Son, born of woman, born under the law, to redeem those who were under the law, so that we might receive adoption as sons. And because you are sons, God has sent the Spirit of his Son into our hearts, crying, "Abba! Father!" **Galatians 3:6-14** — Know then that it is those of faith who are the sons of Abraham. And the Scripture, foreseeing that God would justify the Gentiles by faith, preached the Gospel beforehand to Abraham, saying, "In you shall all the nations be blessed." So then, those who are of faith are blessed along with Abraham, the man of faith. For all who rely on works of the law are under a curse; for it is written, "Cursed be everyone who does not abide by all things written in the Book of the Law and do them." Now it is evident that no one is justified before God by the law, for "The righteous shall live by faith." But the law is not of faith, rather "The one who does them shall live by them." Christ redeemed us from the curse of the law by becoming a curse for us—for it is written, "Cursed is everyone who is hanged on a tree"— so that in Christ Jesus the blessing of Abraham might come to the Gentiles, so that we might receive the promised Spirit through faith. **2Corinthians 5:21** — For our sake he made him to be sin who knew no sin, so that in him we might become the righteousness of God. **John 1:14, 16-18** —And the Word became flesh and dwelt among us, and we have seen his glory, glory as of the only Son from the Father, full of grace and truth. ...For from his fullness we have all received, grace upon grace. For the law was given through Moses; grace and truth came through Jesus Christ. No one has ever seen God; the only God, who is at the Father's side, he has made him known.

16. The second incarnation: Christ within me, forming His Life in me

After His death, resurrection, and ascension, the Father sent the Holy Spirit so that all who trust Christ share in a kind of "second incarnation." Jesus is no longer just *with* us, but *within* us, forming us into His likeness. Paul calls this deeply personal mystery "Christ in you, the hope of glory." Through His Spirit, the same Jesus who lived, died, and rose for us now lives in us. He did not come only to stand beside me or accomplish salvation for me from the outside; He came so that the Christ who was for me would now be in me, uniting me to Himself in a shared, living union. This does not make me divine; it means the living God has chosen to dwell in my real, everyday humanity—my personality, my history, my very body—making it His temple. **Through this union, my life is hidden with Christ in God, and Christ shares His own life with me from the inside—not as an occasional guest, but as a permanent, loving Presence.** His story becomes the truest story of my life, and my life becomes a place where His life is made visible. The same Jesus who once walked the dusty roads of Galilee now walks through my everyday life—not merely beside me, but within me—so that, as I trust Him, He steadily forms His life in me, reshaping my desires, thoughts, and choices from the inside out.

Colossians 1:27 —"...God chose to make known...this mystery...which is Christ in you, the hope of glory." **Colossians 3:3** – For you have died, and your life is hidden with Christ in God. **Romans 8:9–10** —You, however, are not in the flesh but in the Spirit, if in fact the Spirit of God dwells in you. Anyone who does not have the Spirit of Christ does not belong to him. But if Christ is in you, although the body is dead because of sin, the Spirit is life because of righteousness. If the Spirit of him who raised Jesus from the dead dwells in you, he who raised Christ Jesus from the dead will also give life to your mortal bodies through his Spirit who dwells in you. **John 14:16–20** – And I will ask the Father, and he will give you another Helper, to be with you forever, even the Spirit of truth, whom the world cannot receive, because it neither sees him nor knows him. You know him, for he dwells with you and will be in you. "I will not leave you as orphans; I will come to you. Yet a little while and the world will see me no more, but you will see me. Because I live, you also will live. In that day you will know that I am in my Father, and you in me, and I in you. **Ephesians 3:16-19** – [I pray] that according to the riches of his glory he may grant you to be strengthened with power through his Spirit in your inner being, so that Christ may dwell in your hearts through faith—that you, being rooted and grounded in love, may have strength to comprehend with all the saints what is the breadth and length and height and depth, and to know (*experientially*) the love of Christ that surpasses (*factual*) knowledge, that you may be filled with all the fullness of God.

17. The normal Christian life

Seen this way, the "abiding life" Jesus described and the "in Christ / Christ in you" life Paul proclaimed are not two different paths, but one and the same life viewed from different angles. Because of the double incarnation—Christ *with* me in His first coming and Christ *within* me now by His Spirit—the normal Christian life is far more than rule-keeping or sin-management. It is a life in which I increasingly discover that "to live is Christ": Christ as my life, Christ as my righteousness, Christ as the pattern and purpose of my days. **He rescues me not only from the penalty of sin in the future, but from the power and misery of sin in the present**, as His indwelling life becomes the source of my transformation. This does not erase my personality or responsibility; it re-centers them, so that my studies, work, relationships, and rest are no longer separate compartments, but arenas in which the indwelling Christ expresses His life through me for the sake of others. As I learn to trust this reality, "for me to live is Christ" becomes not just a verse to quote, but a confession to inhabit day by day.

Philippians 1:21 – For to me to live is Christ, and to die is gain. **Galatians 2:20** – I have been crucified with Christ. It is no longer I who live, but Christ who lives in me. And the life I now live in the flesh I live by faith in the Son of God, who loved me and gave himself for me. **Romans 8:9–11** – You, however, are not in the flesh but in the Spirit, if in fact the Spirit of God dwells in you. Anyone who does not have the Spirit of Christ does not belong to him. But if Christ is in you, although the body is dead because of sin, the Spirit is life because of righteousness. If the Spirit of him who raised Jesus from the dead dwells in you, he who raised Christ Jesus from the dead will also give life to your mortal bodies through his Spirit who dwells in you.

18. From outside-in religion to inside-out life

Before I understood the Gospel, I naturally gravitated toward an outside-in religion, trying to secure God's favor by keeping rules, trying harder to do better, managing appearances, and comparing myself to others. Even as a believer, my heart still drifts back toward this "both-and" mindset—Jesus plus my performance—as if grace needed to be balanced by law. But God exposes this as a "deadly leaven" that turns good news into slavery. The Spirit now calls me to an inside-out life, where change flows from faith in what Christ has already done and what He is now doing in me. **The law no longer functions as a ladder I climb to reach God; instead, the Spirit writes God's ways on my heart**, producing obedience as the joyful fruit of a relationship already secured by grace. I like to remember it this way: Jesus plus anything equals nothing; Jesus plus nothing equals everything.

Galatians 3:1–5 — O foolish Galatians! Who has bewitched you? It was before your eyes that Jesus Christ was publicly portrayed as crucified. Let me ask you only this: Did you receive the Spirit by works of the law or by hearing with faith? Are you so foolish? Having begun by the Spirit, are you now being perfected by the flesh? Did you suffer so many things in vain—if indeed it was in vain? Does he who supplies the Spirit to you and works miracles among you do so by works of the law, or by hearing with faith? **Galatians 5:1–5**— For freedom Christ has set us free; stand firm therefore, and do not submit again to a yoke of slavery. ...For through the Spirit, by faith, we ourselves eagerly wait for the hope of righteousness. For in Christ Jesus neither circumcision nor uncircumcision counts for anything, but only faith working through love. **Romans 7:4–6** – Likewise, my brothers, you also have died to the law through the body of Christ, so that you may belong to another, to him who has been raised from the dead, in order that we may bear fruit for God. For while we were living in the flesh, our sinful passions, aroused by the law, were at work in our members to bear fruit for death. But now we are released from the law, having died to that which held us captive, so that we serve in the new way of the Spirit and not in the old way of the written code. **Jeremiah 31:31–34** – "Behold, the days are coming, declares the LORD, when I will make a new covenant with the house of Israel and the house of Judah, not like the covenant that I made with their fathers on the day when I took them by the hand to bring them out of the land of Egypt, my covenant that they broke, though I was their husband, declares the LORD. For this is the covenant that I will make with the house of Israel after those days, declares the LORD: I will put my law within them, and I will write it on their hearts. And I will be their God, and they shall be my people. And no longer shall each one teach his neighbor and each his brother, saying, 'Know the LORD,' for they shall all know me, from the least of them to the greatest, declares the LORD. For I will forgive their iniquity, and I will remember their sin no more."

19. My old self crucified with Christ

At the cross, something happened not only outside of me but also to me. My old self—the person I was in Adam: condemned, law-measured, approval-hungry, shaped by sin and shame—was crucified with Christ, so that it is no longer the truest definition of who I am. Sin still pulls at my heart and shows up in my thoughts and desires, but I am no longer its slave. The person who was bound under the curse of the law has, in God's reckoning, died. This means I do not fight sin as a prisoner begging for parole, but as someone who has already been transferred into a new realm of grace. **The more I reckon myself dead to sin and alive to God in Christ Jesus, the more my lived experience begins to line up with what is already true of me in Him**.

Romans 6:6–11 —We know that our old self was crucified with him in order that the body of sin might be brought to nothing, so that we would no longer be enslaved to sin. For one who has died has been set free from sin. Now if we have died with Christ, we believe that we will also live with him. We know that Christ, being raised from the dead, will never die again; death no longer has dominion over him. For the death he died he died to sin, once for all, but the life he lives he lives to God. So, you also must consider yourselves dead to sin and alive to God in Christ Jesus. **Colossians 3:1-4** —If then you have been raised with Christ, seek the things that are above, where Christ is, seated at the right hand of God. Set your minds on things that are above, not on things that are on earth. For you have died, and your life is hidden with Christ in God. When Christ who is your life appears, then you also will appear with him in glory.

20. I no longer live the life I live

When Paul says, "It is no longer I who live, but Christ lives in me," he is not saying that he ceased to exist or became a generic Christian personality. He means that the old, sin-ruled self that tried to live apart from God has been crucified with Christ, and that his whole life is now centered in the Son of God who loved him and gave Himself for him. Paul is still very much Paul—with his own story, temperament, gifts, and voice—but the deepest "I" of his life has shifted from "me in myself" to "me in Christ." Union with Christ does not erase my God-given personality or turn me into an echo of everyone else. In Christ, I am freed from sin's distortion so that I can become more truly the person God created me to be. The Spirit redeems my particular history, wiring, and gifting so that Jesus can express His life through me in a way no one else can. So when I confess, "It is no longer I who live, but Christ lives in me," I am not denying who I am; I am learning to live my ordinary, embodied life by faith in the

Son of God who now lives in me. And, His life in me is never meant to stop with me. The same Christ lives in *us*, forming a people in whom His one life is expressed through many different stories, temperaments, and gifts. In the body of Christ, I am freed not only to be the real, redeemed "me" in Him, but also to delight in the particular ways He lives through others—ways that are not exactly like me at all. **Jesus, live Your life in me so that I become more truly myself in You—my true, redeemed self—for the sake of others**.

Galatians 2:20 – I have been crucified with Christ. It is no longer I who live, but Christ who lives in me. And the life I now live in the flesh I live by faith in the Son of God, who loved me and gave himself for me. **2 Corinthians 4:7–11** – But we have this treasure in jars of clay, to show that the surpassing power belongs to God and not to us. We are afflicted in every way but not crushed; perplexed but not driven to despair; persecuted but not forsaken; struck down but not destroyed; always carrying in the body the death of Jesus, so that the life of Jesus may also be manifested in our bodies. For we who live are always being given over to death for Jesus' sake, so that the life of Jesus also may be manifested in our mortal flesh. **Colossians 3:3–4** – For you have died, and your life is hidden with Christ in God. When Christ who is your life appears, then you also will appear with him in glory.

21. Walking by the Spirit

To "walk by the Spirit" is to live each moment in conscious dependence on the indwelling Christ rather than on my flesh—my old patterns of self-salvation, self-promotion, and self-protection. This walk is not primarily about chasing experiences; it is about trusting a Person, which is itself deeply experiential, as His Spirit makes Jesus' abiding love more real to my heart—not merely as a doctrine I affirm, but as a lived experience of His love that surpasses knowledge. The Spirit is not a vague force but a Person—the very presence of Jesus in me, making His love real to my heart moment by moment. He does not merely guide me from outside; He shapes me from within, bending my desires toward the things Jesus loves. As I look to Him in the concrete details of my day—temptations, conversations, decisions—the Spirit leads me away from the old scripts of the flesh and into the new scripts of Jesus' life in me. The result is not sinless perfection, but a growing pattern in which His desires increasingly shape my choices, and the works of the flesh lose their grip, not because I have become strong, but because the life of Jesus in me is flowing through me. **Walking by the Spirit, then, is not my way of qualifying for God's favor, but the way I enjoy the favor already secured for me in Jesus.**

Galatians 5:16–18 — But I say, walk by the Spirit, and you will not gratify the desires of the flesh. For the desires of the flesh are against the Spirit, and the desires of the Spirit are against the flesh, for these are opposed to each other, to keep you from doing the things you want to do. But if you are led by the Spirit, you are not under the law. **Galatians 5:22–25** — But the fruit of the Spirit is love, joy, peace, patience, kindness, goodness, faithfulness, gentleness, self-control; against such things there is no law. And those who belong to Christ Jesus have crucified the flesh with its passions and desires. If we live by the Spirit, let us also keep in step with the Spirit. **Romans 8:4–6** — in order that the righteous requirement of the law might be fulfilled in us, who walk not according to the flesh but according to the Spirit. For those who live according to the flesh set their minds on the things of the flesh, but those who live according to the Spirit set their minds on the things of the Spirit. For to set the mind on the flesh is death, but to set the mind on the Spirit is life and peace. **Romans 8:13–14** —For if you live according to the flesh you will die, but if by the Spirit you put to death the deeds of the body, you will live. For all who are led by the Spirit of God are sons of God. **John 15:7** — If you abide in me, and my words abide in you, ask whatever you wish, and it will be done for you. **Ephesians 3:16–19**— that according to the riches of his glory he may grant you to be strengthened with power through his Spirit in your inner being, so that Christ may dwell in your hearts through faith—that you, being rooted and grounded in love, may have the strength to comprehend with all the saint what is the breadth and length and height and depth, and to know (*experientially*) the love of Christ that surpasses (*factual*) knowledge, that you may be filled with all the fullness of God.

22. Rescued from this present evil age

When Christ gave Himself for my sins, He did it "to rescue me from this present evil age," not merely to secure my place in heaven when I die. The Gospel is not only deliverance from future judgment; it is a rescue from the enslaving systems, idols, and false Gospels that shape the world around me. Whether I once trusted in cultural idols or in religious performance, Jesus has broken the spell of those "gods" by showing Himself more beautiful and more sufficient. This means **I am free not only from the wrath to come, but from the crushing need to find my worth in what this age exalts—success, image, control, or even religious pride**. I am no longer enslaved by what everyone around me chases or fears losing; my life is no longer defined by the rise and fall of my reputation, productivity, or position. Because I have been rescued, I am free to seek first His kingdom, even when this age calls that foolish. I now belong to the age to come, even as I follow Him in the midst of this one.

Galatians 1:3–4 – Grace to you and peace from God our Father and the Lord Jesus Christ, who gave himself for our sins to deliver us from the present evil age, according to the will of our God and Father. **Galatians 4:8–9** – Formerly, when you did not know God, you were enslaved to those that by nature are not gods. But now that you have come to know God, or rather to be known by God, how can you turn back again to the weak and worthless elementary principles of the world, whose slaves you want to be once more? **Romans 12:1–2** – I appeal to you therefore, brothers, by the mercies of God, to present your bodies as a living sacrifice, holy and acceptable to God, which is your spiritual worship. Do not be conformed to this world, but be transformed by the renewal of your mind, that by testing you may discern what is the will of God, what is good and acceptable and perfect. **Colossians 1:13–14** – He has delivered us from the domain of darkness and transferred us to the kingdom of his beloved Son, in whom we have redemption, the forgiveness of sins.

23. Free from guilt and the treadmill of performance

Because God has justified me in Christ, there is now no condemnation for me—no guilty verdict left hanging over my life. **When I sin,**

my conscience may accuse me, and the enemy may shame me, but God's gavel has already fallen in my favor because Jesus bore my sentence on the cross. This frees me from the treadmill of trying to prove my worth to God or to others through constant striving. Instead of cycling between pride when I "perform well" and despair when I fail, I can return again and again to the solid ground of Christ's righteousness, confessing my sin honestly and enjoying a fresh experience of the cleansing that has already been secured by His blood.

Romans 8:1-4 – There is therefore now no condemnation for those who are in Christ Jesus. For the law of the Spirit of life has set you free in Christ Jesus from the law of sin and death. For God has done what the law, weakened by the flesh, could not do. By sending his own Son in the likeness of sinful flesh and for sin, he condemned sin in the flesh, in order that the righteous requirement of the law might be fulfilled in us, who walk not according to the flesh but according to the Spirit. **Romans 5:1-2** – Therefore, since we have been justified by faith, we have peace with God through our Lord Jesus Christ. Through him we have also obtained access by faith into this grace in which we stand, and we rejoice in hope of the glory of God. **Galatians 3:1-3** – O foolish Galatians! Who has bewitched you? It was before your eyes that Jesus Christ was publicly portrayed as crucified. Let me ask you only this: Did you receive the Spirit by works of the law or by hearing with faith? Are you so foolish? Having begun by the Spirit, are you now being perfected by the flesh? **1 John 1:7–9** – But if we walk in the light, as he is in the light, we have fellowship with one another, and the blood of Jesus his Son cleanses us from all sin. If we say we have no sin, we deceive ourselves, and the truth is not in us. If we confess our sins, he is faithful and just to forgive us our sins and to cleanse us from all unrighteousness.

24. Grace as the engine of change

The grace that justifies me apart from works is the same grace that now empowers me to live differently—not by adding law to Gospel, but by letting the Spirit train my heart to say "No" to ungodliness and "Yes" to a life that reflects His character. If I try to "balance" grace with law as the basis of my standing with God, I fall from a grace-based way of salvation back into a law-based system of earning, and the joy drains out of my obedience. But when I see Christ crucified clearly portrayed for me, my heart is softened, my defenses lower, and I find myself wanting to please the One who loved me and gave Himself for me. In that way, **grace does what law never could: it changes me from the inside**

out, making obedience a response of love rather than a strategy for self-salvation.

Ephesians 2:8 – For by grace you have been saved through faith. And this is not your own doing; it is the gift of God. **Galatians 3:1–5** – O foolish Galatians! Who has bewitched you? It was before your eyes that Jesus Christ was publicly portrayed as crucified. Let me ask you only this: Did you receive the Spirit by works of the law or by hearing with faith? Are you so foolish? Having begun by the Spirit, are you now being perfected by the flesh? Did you suffer so many things in vain—if indeed it was in vain? Does he who supplies the Spirit to you and works miracles among you do so by works of the law, or by hearing with faith? **Galatians 5:4–6** – You are severed from Christ, you who would be justified by the law; you have fallen away from grace. For through the Spirit, by faith, we ourselves eagerly wait for the hope of righteousness. For in Christ Jesus neither circumcision nor uncircumcision counts for anything, but only faith working through love. **Titus 2:11–14** –For the grace of God has appeared, bringing salvation for all people, training us to renounce ungodliness and worldly passions, and to live self-controlled, upright, and godly lives in the present age, waiting for our blessed hope, the appearing of the glory of our great God and Savior Jesus Christ, who gave himself for us to redeem us from all lawlessness and to purify for himself a people for his own possession who are zealous for good works. **Romans 11:6** – But if it is by grace, it is no longer on the basis of works; otherwise, grace would no longer be grace.

25. Christ being formed in me

Christ lives in me—right now, fully and forever. This is the stunning truth of the Gospel: united to Jesus by faith, the eternal Son dwells in me by His Spirit. This indwelling is a finished reality—nothing can undo it. Yet it's meant to unfold and show itself more and more in my everyday life. Christ in me wants to live His life through me. As that reality grows, my thoughts line up more with His mind, my affections mirror what moves His heart, my choices reflect His wisdom and obedience, and my actions carry more of His grace and truth. I start to look, sound, and act more like Jesus—not by trying harder in my own strength, but because His life presses outward from within. Paul prayed earnestly "until Christ is formed" in his spiritual children. Spiritual formation isn't instant; it's gradual. The inner reality of Christ in me increasingly shapes how I live. I may stumble, feel the pull of old fleshly patterns, or get discouraged by slow change. But **the life of Jesus is already in me, and He doesn't quit. He keeps renewing my mind and forming Himself in me until more of who He is shows up in who I am**.

Galatians 4:19 – My little children, for whom I am again in the anguish of childbirth until Christ is formed in you! **Romans 8:29** –For those whom he foreknew he also predestined to be conformed to the image of his Son, in order that he might be the firstborn among many brothers. **2 Corinthians 3:18** – And we all, with unveiled face, beholding the glory of the Lord, are being transformed into the same image from one degree of glory to another. For this comes from the Lord who is the Spirit. **Philippians 1:6** – And I am sure of this, that he who began a good work in you will bring it to completion at the day of Jesus Christ. **Romans 12:1–2** – I appeal to you therefore, brothers, by the mercies of God, to present your bodies as a living sacrifice, holy and acceptable to God, which is your spiritual worship. Do not be conformed to this world, but be transformed by the renewal of your mind, that by testing you may discern what is the will of God, what is good and acceptable and perfect.

26. Spiritual formation as the Spirit's work

Spiritual formation is not my self-improvement project; it is the Spirit's life-long artistry, using every season to conform me to Christ. He works in me both to will and to act according to God's good purpose, engaging my choices without negating my dependence. Seasons of apparent stagnation, wilderness, or even regression do not mean He has abandoned His work in me; often they are the very places where He deepens my roots and exposes my false trusts. **My role is not to anxiously monitor my own progress, but to keep presenting myself to God, abiding in His Word, staying connected to His people, and enjoying His presence, trusting that He who began a good work in me will carry it on to completion in the day of Christ Jesus.**

Philippians 2:12–13 – Therefore, my beloved, as you have always obeyed, so now, not only as in my presence but much more in my absence, work out your own salvation with fear and trembling, for it is God who works in you, both to will and to work for his good pleasure. **Philippians 1:6** – And I am sure of this, that he who began a good work in you will bring it to completion at the day of Jesus Christ. **Hebrews 13:20–21** – Now may the God of peace who brought again from the dead our Lord Jesus, the great shepherd of the sheep, by the blood of the eternal covenant, equip you with everything good that you may do his will, working in us that which is pleasing in his sight, through Jesus Christ, to whom be glory forever and ever. Amen. **Romans 12:1** – I appeal to you therefore, brothers, by the mercies of God, to present your bodies as a living sacrifice, holy and acceptable to God, which is your spiritual worship.

27. Free to love, not to indulge

Christ has set me free from the curse of the law and from a rule-based approach to God, but this freedom is not a license for self-centered living. If I use my freedom merely to gratify my flesh, I drift back into the very slavery from which I was rescued, and my relationships begin to devour themselves. The Spirit teaches me a better way: to use my freedom to serve others through love. **When I lay down my rights for the good of another, I am not losing freedom; I am stepping into the very life of Christ.** In those moments, love—not my desires—gets the final say. In doing so, I discover that real freedom is not the absence of all constraint, but the ability to live in the way I was created—to love God with all my heart and my neighbor as myself, in the One who lives and abides in me.

Galatians 5:1 —For freedom Christ has set us free; stand firm therefore, and do not submit again to a yoke of slavery. **Galatians 5:13–15** — For you were called to freedom, brothers. Only do not use your freedom as an opportunity for the flesh, but through love serve one another. For the whole law is fulfilled in one word: "You shall love your neighbor as yourself." But if you bite and devour one another, watch out that you are not consumed by one another. **Romans 6:15–18** — What then? Are we to sin because we are not under law but under grace? By no means! Do you not know that if you present yourselves to anyone as obedient slaves, you are slaves of the one whom you obey, either of sin, which leads to death, or of obedience, which leads to righteousness? But thanks be to God, that you who were once slaves of sin have become obedient from the heart to the standard of teaching to which you were committed, and, having been set free from sin, have become slaves of righteousness. **1 Peter 2:16** – Live as people who are free, not using your freedom as a cover-up for evil, but living as servants of God.

28. Love fulfilling the law through me

When Christ's love takes deeper hold of my heart, the very law that once condemned me is now fulfilled through me. The whole law is summed up in this: "You shall love your neighbor as yourself," and this is precisely what the Spirit produces as He pours God's love into my heart. I will never keep God's commands perfectly in this life, yet as His love moves me to forgive, to welcome, to speak truth, and to seek others' good, I find myself walking in the very path the law was always pointing toward. **Love does what fear cannot: it moves me beyond mere rule-keeping into a life of love that truly reflects the heart of God.**

Romans 5:5 – and hope does not put us to shame, because God's love has been poured into our hearts through the Holy Spirit who has been given to us. **Galatians 5:14** – For the whole law is fulfilled in one word: "You shall love your neighbor as yourself." — **Romans 13:8–10** — Owe no one anything, except to love each other, for the one who loves another has fulfilled the law. For the commandments, "You shall not commit adultery, You shall not murder, You shall not steal, You shall not covet," and any other commandment, are summed up in this word: "You shall love your neighbor as yourself." Love does no wrong to a neighbor; therefore, love is the fulfilling of the law. **1 John 4:7–12** — Beloved, let us love one another, for love is from God, and whoever loves has been born of God and knows God. Anyone who does not love does not know God, because God is love. In this the love of God was made manifest among us, that God sent his only Son into the world, so that we might live through him. In this is love, not that we have loved God but that he loved us and sent his Son to be the propitiation for our sins. Beloved, if God so loved us, we also ought to love one another. No one has ever seen God; if we love one another, God abides in us and his love is perfected in us.

Thoughts & Observations

Part III

(Days 29-42)

Jesus in Me, Living Through Me, For the Sake of Others

As Jesus lives in me and among us, His indwelling presence meets us in ordinary days, relationships, weakness, trials, and mission, so that together we learn to abide in Him, in His word, and in His love – for the sake of others.

29. The fruit of the Spirit is the abiding life made visible

As was said earlier, the fruit of the Spirit is the outward expression of the inward abiding life of Christ. Love, where I once nursed resentment; **joy**, amid disappointment peace, in the face of uncertainty; patience, with people who used to drive me crazy—these are not natural upgrades; they are signs that Jesus is living in me. This fruit grows gradually, like grapes on a vine. My task is not to stare anxiously at the branches, but to stay rooted in Jesus through His Word, prayer, and dependence. As I do, **the Spirit quietly ripens His fruit, turning my life into a living testimony that Christ truly dwells in His people.** The fruit is not my proof of worthiness; it is the Spirit's quiet testimony that grace is at work in someone already fully loved. And because we abide together, this fruit is meant to ripen in our shared life as a church so that our "one another" love becomes the most visible cluster on the vine, and joy is the sweetness of our abiding lives. (*See page 124 for more on joy.*)

John 15:5 — I am the vine; you are the branches. Whoever abides in me and I in him, he it is that bears much fruit, for apart from me you can do nothing. **John 15:8** – By this my Father is glorified, that you bear much fruit and so prove to be my disciples. **Galatians 5:22–23** – But the fruit of the Spirit is love, joy, peace, patience, kindness, goodness, faithfulness, gentleness, self-control; against such things there is no law. **Philippians 1:9–11** – And it is my prayer that your love may abound more and more, with knowledge and all discernment, so that you may approve what is excellent, and so be pure and blameless for the day of Christ, filled with the fruit of righteousness that comes through Jesus Christ, to the glory and praise of God. **John 15:11** – These things I have spoken to you, that my joy may be in you and that your joy may be full.

30. Jesus living through me in my relationships

Abiding is never merely private; the life of Christ in me is meant to overflow into every relationship He has entrusted to me. *In my home,* He wants to love my spouse, children, or roommates through me; *in my church,* He wants to bear with others' weaknesses and forgive offenses through me. Abiding together means forgiving as we've been forgiven, speaking truth in love, and carrying one another's burdens—practices that make Christ's life tangible in our "one another" life. *In my workplace and neighborhood,* He wants to show patience, integrity, and compassion through me. Incarnational reality means that Christ in me reaches out in love even to those who have wounded me, so that forgiveness and mercy flow from that deep center where He and I share life together. I am not merely trying harder to follow His example; my whole self—mind, emotions, body—becomes an instrument through which His love can move. When I feel inadequate for this calling—as I often do—I remember that I am a branch, not the Vine; **my job is not to manufacture Christlike relationships, but to abide in Jesus and let His love, wisdom, and courage flow through my words, my listening, and my presence**. In laughter with friends, in the simple pleasure of being known, Jesus is not absent but present; delighting in us as we delight in one another. The joy of ordinary friendship is a foretaste of the feast to come, and it is holy.

John 15:4–5 – Abide in me, and I in you… I am the vine; you are the branches. **John 13:34–35** – "Just as I have loved you, you also are to love one another. By this all people will know that you are my disciples…" **Galatians 6:2** – Bear one another's burdens and so fulfill the law of Christ. **Ephesians 4:15–16** – Speaking the truth in love, we are to grow up in every way into him who is the head, into Christ... **Colossians 3:12-14** – Put on then... compassionate hearts, kindness, humility, meekness, and patience, bearing with one another and... forgiving each other... And above all these, put on love, which binds everything together in perfect harmony.

31. Jesus living through me in failure and weakness

My failures and weaknesses do not disqualify me from the abiding life; they are often the very places where I experience it most deeply. When I blow it—again—in an area I thought I had mastered, the old scripts of shame and self-condemnation rush in, telling me that God must be angry with me. The Gospel tells another story: the One who lives in me is the crucified and risen Savior who intercedes for me, and **my weakness becomes a stage on which His strength can be displayed**. Sometimes the weakness is not failure but simply suffering—the mysterious weight of sorrow, loss, or pain that I did not choose and cannot explain. In those moments, abiding may look less like confident trust and more like honest lament. The Psalms give voice to this: "My God, my God, why have you forsaken me?" "Darkness has become my only companion." Jesus Himself cried out in anguish, and His tears teach me that bringing my real grief to the Father is not a failure of faith but a form of staying near. As I bring my failure or my sorrow into the light, trusting His finished work rather than my own performance, He meets me with mercy, restores me, and often uses these humbling experiences to soften my heart toward others who share similar struggles. And when I am honest about my weakness with my brothers and sisters, my failure becomes not just a place of personal restoration but a bridge of compassion to others who need the same grace.

2 Corinthians 12:9–10 – But he said to me, "My grace is sufficient for you, for my power is made perfect in weakness." Therefore, I will boast all the more gladly of my weaknesses, so that the power of Christ may rest upon me. For the sake of Christ, then, I am content with weaknesses, insults, hardships, persecutions, and calamities. For when I am weak, then I am strong. **Romans 5:20–21** – Now the law came in to increase the trespass, but where sin increased, grace abounded all the more, so that, as sin reigned in death, grace also might reign through righteousness leading to eternal life through Jesus Christ our Lord. **1John 1:7–2:2** – But if we walk in the light, as he is in the light, we have fellowship with one another, and the blood of Jesus his Son cleanses us from all sin. If we say we have no sin, we deceive ourselves, and the truth is not in us. If we confess our sins, he is faithful and just to forgive us our sins and to cleanse us from all unrighteousness. If we say we have not sinned, we make him a liar, and his word is not in us. My little children, I am writing these things to you so that you may not sin. But if anyone does sin, we have an advocate with the Father, Jesus Christ the righteous. He is the propitiation for our sins, and not for ours only but also for the sins of the whole world.

32. Jesus living through me in opportunity and risk

Not only in weakness, but also in new opportunities and risks, the abiding Christ wants to live His life through me. When He calls me into something that feels beyond my capacity—a hard conversation, a step of generosity, a new ministry, a costly act of obedience—my flesh either shrinks back in fear or surges ahead in self-confidence. The Spirit invites me into a third way: honest acknowledgment of my weakness, combined with confident trust in Christ's sufficiency within me. **As I step forward depending on Him, I often discover that He has gone ahead of me, preparing the way and supplying what I lacked.**

1 Corinthians 2:3–5 —And I was with you in weakness and in fear and much trembling, and my speech and my message were not in plausible words of wisdom, but in demonstration of the Spirit and of power, so that your faith might not rest in the wisdom of men but in the power of God. **Joshua 1:9** – Have I not commanded you? Be strong and courageous. Do not be frightened, and do not be dismayed, for the LORD your God is with you wherever you go. **Ephesians 3:20–21** Now to him who is able to do far more abundantly than all that we ask or think, according to the power at work within us, to him be glory in the church and in Christ Jesus throughout all generations, forever and ever. Amen. **Hebrews 13:20–21** – Now may the God of peace who brought again from the dead our Lord Jesus, the great shepherd of the sheep, by the blood of the eternal covenant, equip you with everything good that you may do his will, working in us that which is pleasing in his sight, through Jesus Christ, to whom be glory forever and ever. Amen.

33. Jesus living through me in the mundane and monotonous

Most of my life is not lived in dramatic highs or devastating lows, but in the ordinary routines of work, chores, errands, and small conversations. The abiding life means that Jesus is just as present and active in these mundane moments as He is in crises or mountaintop experiences. When I fold laundry, answer emails, sit in traffic, or shop for groceries with a heart turned toward Him, these tasks become places of quiet worship and hidden fruitfulness. Over time, these unseen moments of "ordinary faithfulness" do more to shape my character than rare, spiritual highs. In the slow, repetitive hours where no one is applauding, He trains my heart to listen, to give thanks, and to love the person right in front of me. **Christ's life in me dignifies the ordinary, transforming "whatever you do" into opportunities to do all in His name and for His glory, even when no one else notices**.

Colossians 3:17 —And whatever you do, in word or deed, do everything in the name of the Lord Jesus, giving thanks to God the Father through him. **Colossians 3:23–24** – Whatever you do, work heartily, as for the Lord and not for men, knowing that from the Lord you will receive the inheritance as your reward. You are serving the Lord Christ. **1 Corinthians 10:31** – So, whether you eat or drink, or whatever you do, do all to the glory of God.

34. From God-amnesia to God-awareness

Though Christ lives in me, my awareness of Him easily drifts; I move through hours as if I were alone, living in a kind of functional atheism or "God-amnesia." Practicing the presence of God is not about conjuring Him up, but about directing and redirecting my mind to the One who is already here, the indwelling Christ whose incarnational reality fills the deepest recesses of my being. Simple habits—brief prayers, breath-prayers, recalling a verse, imagining Jesus beside me in conversations—help me set the Lord continually before me and become more and more aware of His presence in me. **Over time, this gentle returning of my attention becomes a way of life, and I begin to discover that joy, peace, guidance, and even quiet intuitions from the Spirit flow not primarily from my circumstances changing, but from a growing awareness that He is with me and within me** in all of them. So, I return again and again—not to make Him present, but to live awake to the Presence that never leaves me.

Psalm 16:8–9 – I have set the LORD always before me; because he is at my right hand, I shall not be shaken. Therefore, my heart is glad, and my whole being rejoices; my flesh also dwells secure. **Psalm 62:1** – For God alone my soul waits in silence; from him comes my salvation. **1 Thessalonians 5:17** – pray without ceasing. **John 14:16–17** – And I will ask the Father, and he will give you another Helper, to be with you forever, even the Spirit of truth, whom the world cannot receive, because it neither sees him nor knows him. You know him, for he dwells with you and will be in you.

35. Silent prayer as resting in the One who lives in me

In a world of constant noise and hurry, silent prayer becomes a powerful practice of abiding. When I sit in stillness before God, I am not trying to impress Him with eloquence or convince Him to act; **in silence, I stop talking, stop asking, stop striving, and simply rest in the presence of Christ who is already within me.** Thoughts will wander, distractions will intrude, and that is okay; each time my mind wanders, I simply return to Him—perhaps with a simple phrase like "Here I am, Lord," or "You are my refuge." Over time, this quiet sitting helps me move from living in my head to living from my heart, where Christ is. It trains my soul to be at home with God, so that even in busy hours I can more easily sink back into that inner room where we abide together. *(See page 102 to learn more about the practice of silence and solitude.)*

Psalm 62:1–2 – For God alone my soul waits in silence; from him comes my salvation. He alone is my rock and my salvation, my fortress; I shall not be greatly shaken. **Psalm 62:5** – For God alone, O my soul, wait in silence, for my hope is from him. **Psalm 46:10** – Be still and know that I am God. I will be exalted among the nations; I will be exalted in the earth! **Isaiah 30:15** – In returning and rest, you shall be saved; in quietness and trust, shall be your strength.

36. Slow, Spirit-guided Scripture reading as abiding in His Word

Abiding in Christ and abiding in His Word go together. When I race through Scripture merely to gather information or check a box, I easily slide into a Christianity that is mostly about facts and ideas rather than living contact with the incarnate God. Incarnational reality means I do not come to the Bible as a detached observer, but as one in whom the Author Himself dwells, ready to speak to me through the text by His Spirit. When I read slowly, prayerfully, and with imagination—asking the Holy Spirit to make God's Word in the text become God's Word in me—I begin to encounter Jesus Himself in the stories and teachings of Scripture, and His words start to live in me, shaping my perspectives and reactions. **A single phrase, carried through the day, can become a thread of grace, wrapping around my thoughts and drawing them back to Him.** *(See page 105 for more about the practice of "Spirit-Guided, Gospel-Meditation.)*

John 8:31-32 — If you abide in my Word, you are truly my disciples, and you will know the truth, and the truth will set you free. **John 15:7** – If you abide in me, and my words abide in you, ask whatever you wish, and it will be done for you. **Psalm 1:1–3** – Blessed is the man who walks not in the counsel of the wicked, nor stands in the way of sinners, nor sits in the seat of scoffers; but his delight is in the law of the LORD, and on his law he meditates day and night. He is like a tree planted by streams of water that yields its fruit in its season, and its leaf does not wither. In all that he does, he prospers. **Hebrews 4:12** –For the word of God is living and active, sharper than any two-edged sword, piercing to the division of soul and of spirit, of joints and of marrow, and discerning the thoughts and intentions of the heart. **Luke 24:27** – And beginning with Moses and all the Prophets, he interpreted to them in all the Scriptures the things concerning himself. **Luke 24:32** – They said to each other, "Did not our hearts burn within us while he talked to us on the road, while he opened to us the Scriptures?" **Luke 24:45** – Then he opened their minds to understand the Scriptures.

37. My daily confession

Each day I wake up tempted to live as if it all depends on me. A simple daily confession can re-align my heart with the abiding life: "**Jesus, You live in me, to live Your life through me, for the sake of others. I invite you to live through me right here, right now.**" In praying this, I am not asking Him to come to me from far away, but I am acknowledging His presence both with me and within me. I am inviting His active lordship over my thoughts, words, and actions. I can repeat this confession before a meeting, a hard conversation, a time of temptation, or a mundane task; it is a practical response to the Spirit's quiet witness that Jesus resides within me. It becomes an act of faith, a way of "reckoning" myself alive to God in Christ and dead to sin, shifting the weight of my day from my shoulders to His.

Galatians 2:20 – I have been crucified with Christ. It is no longer I who live, but Christ who lives in me. And the life I now live in the flesh I live by faith in the Son of God, who loved me and gave himself for me. **Romans 6:11–13** – So, you also must consider yourselves dead to sin and alive to God in Christ Jesus. Let not sin therefore reign in your mortal body to make you obey its passions. Do not present your members to sin as instruments for unrighteousness but present yourselves to God as those who have been brought from death to life, and your members to God as instruments for righteousness. **Romans 12:1–2** – I appeal to you therefore, brothers, by the mercies of God, to present your bodies as a living sacrifice, holy and acceptable to God, which is your spiritual worship. Do not be conformed to this world, but be transformed by the renewal of your mind, that by testing you may discern what is the will of God, what is good and acceptable and perfect.

38. Saying "no" to moral reformation, "yes" to Gospel transformation

There will always be a religious part of me that wants to manage sin by tightening rules, and focusing on behavior modification. While external boundaries have their place, moral reformation alone cannot produce the abiding, Spirit-formed life Jesus died to make possible. The Gospel calls me deeper: to bring my sins and struggles into the light, tracing them down to the false saviors and self-righteousness that drive them, and then to look afresh to Christ crucified and risen for me. **As I repent not only of bad behavior but of the idols beneath it, and as I rest anew in His grace, the Spirit uses the beauty of the Gospel—not the pressure of the law—to change what I love, not just what I do**.

Galatians 5:1-4— For freedom Christ has set us free; stand firm therefore, and do not submit again to a yoke of slavery. Look: I, Paul, say to you that if you accept circumcision, Christ will be of no advantage to you. I testify again to every man who accepts circumcision that he is obligated to keep the whole law. You are severed from Christ, you who would be justified by the law; you have fallen away from grace. **Galatians 3:1-5** — O foolish Galatians! Who has bewitched you? It was before your eyes that Jesus Christ was publicly portrayed as crucified. Let me ask you only this: Did you receive the Spirit by works of the law or by hearing with faith? Are you so foolish? Having begun by the Spirit, are you now being perfected by the flesh? Did you suffer so many things in vain—if indeed it was in vain? Does he who supplies the Spirit to you and works miracles among you do so by works of the law, or by hearing with faith? **Romans 2:4**— Or do you presume on the riches of his kindness and forbearance and patience, not knowing that God's kindness is meant to lead you to repentance? **Matthew 23:25–28**— "Woe to you, scribes and Pharisees, hypocrites! For you clean the outside of the cup and the plate, but inside they are full of greed and self-indulgence. You blind Pharisee! First clean the inside of the cup and the plate, that the outside also may be clean. "Woe to you, scribes and Pharisees, hypocrites! For you are like whitewashed tombs, which outwardly appear beautiful, but within are full of dead people's bones and all uncleanness. So, you also outwardly appear righteous to others, but within you are full of hypocrisy and lawlessness.

39. Seeing trials and pruning as the Father's wise love

When hardships press into my life, my first instinct is often to believe that God is against me or that I have somehow slipped outside His favor. But the image of the Vinedresser teaches me to interpret trials differently: as evidence of the Father's wise, pursuing love. He is not wielding the pruning knife in anger, but in mercy, cutting away what will not ultimately help me bear the fruit of Christlikeness. Often, I only see the pain of what has been removed; He sees the larger harvest that will one day result. Sometimes abiding looks like lament—honest crying out to God when His ways confuse or disappoint me. Jesus Himself cried out in Gethsemane and on the cross. In those moments, I am not failing to abide; I am abiding in the only way possible—clinging to Him even when I cannot understand Him. Lament is not doubt's opposite; it is love's raw language when love's ways are hidden. The Psalms teach me to cry out, to question, to bring my honest anguish to God. This, too, is abiding, staying near enough to tell Him everything. **Trusting this does not make trials easy, but it does mean I can meet them with honest lament and stubborn hope, knowing that my Father is far more committed to my joy and fruitfulness than I am**.

John 15:1-2 — I am the true vine, and my Father is the vinedresser. Every branch in me that does not bear fruit he takes away, and every branch that does bear fruit he prunes, that it may bear more fruit. **Hebrews 12:5-11** — And have you forgotten the exhortation that addresses you as sons? "My son, do not regard lightly the discipline of the Lord, nor be weary when reproved by him. For the Lord disciplines the one he loves and chastises every son whom he receives." It is for discipline that you have to endure. God is treating you as sons. For what son is there whom his father does not discipline? If you are left without discipline, in which all have participated, then you are illegitimate children and not sons. Besides this, we have had earthly fathers who disciplined us and we respected them. Shall we not much more be subject to the Father of spirits and live? For they disciplined us for a short time as it seemed best to them, but he disciplines us for our good, that we may share his holiness. For the moment all discipline seems painful rather than pleasant, but later it yields the peaceful fruit of righteousness to those who have been trained by it. **James 1:2–4** – Count it all joy, my brothers, when you meet trials of various kinds, for you know that the testing of your faith produces steadfastness. And let steadfastness have its full effect, that you may be perfect and complete, lacking in nothing. **Romans 8:28–29** – And we know that for those who love God all things work together for good, for those who are called according to his purpose. For those whom he foreknew he also predestined to be conformed to the image of his Son, in order that he might be the firstborn among many brothers. **Psalm 88:1-2, 6-7, 14, 18** – O LORD, God of my salvation, I cry out day and night before you… You have put me in the depths of the pit, in the regions dark and deep… O LORD, why do you cast my soul away? Why do you hide your face from me?... You have caused my companions to shun me; you have made me a horror to them… My only companion is darkness.

40. Abiding together: Christ in us as His Body

Abiding is deeply personal, but it is never merely individual, because Christ does not just dwell in "me"; He dwells in "us" as His body. The same Spirit who lives in my heart also lives in my brothers and sisters, and He often mediates Christ's presence to me through their encouragement, counsel, correction, and prayers. When we gather around the Word, share our burdens, and serve together, we are not merely doing religious activities; we are participating in the shared life of Christ among his people. My own abiding is strengthened as I walk with others who are learning to abide, and together we are being built up into a living temple where God dwells by his Spirit.

1 Corinthians 3:16 — Do you not know that you are God's temple and that God's Spirit dwells in you? If anyone destroys God's temple, God will destroy him. For God's temple is holy, and you are that temple. **John 15:12–17** — This is my commandment, that you love one another as I have loved you. Greater love has no one than this, that someone lay down his life for his friends. You are my friends if you do what I command you. No longer do I call you servants, for the servant does not know what his master is doing; but I have called you friends, for all that I have heard from my Father I have made known to you. You did not choose me, but I chose you and appointed you that you should go and bear fruit and that your fruit should abide, so that whatever you ask the Father in my name, he may give it to you. These things I command you, so that you will love one another. **Ephesians 2:19–22** – So then you are no longer strangers and aliens, but you are fellow citizens with the saints and members of the household of God, built on the foundation of the apostles and prophets, Christ Jesus himself being the cornerstone, in whom the whole structure, being joined together, grows into a holy temple in the Lord. In him you also are being built together into a dwelling place for God by the Spirit. **Ephesians 4:15–16** – Rather, speaking the truth in love, we are to grow up in every way into him who is the head, into Christ, from whom the whole body, joined and held together by every joint with which it is equipped, when each part is working properly, makes the body grow so that it builds itself up in love. **Galatians 6:2** – Bear one another's burdens and so fulfill the law of Christ.

41. Always on mission: Jesus living His mission through me

The Christ who lives in me is the same Christ who came "to seek and to save the lost" and who sent His disciples to make Him known among the nations. Abiding in Him, "*for the sake of others,"* naturally draws me into His mission—not as an extra burden or a special program, but as the normal overflow of His heart beating through mine. My neighborhood, my workplace, my city—these are not random places. They are the exact spot where the Vine has planted this branch so that the people around me might taste and see that the Lord is good. As I walk in step with the Spirit day by day, He opens my eyes to the people right in front of me: the coworker who seems discouraged, the neighbor I pass on walks, the cashier who looks tired. He gives me simple words of hope, prompts small acts of kindness, and even uses my ordinary story of grace to point others toward Jesus. Living on mission doesn't always look dramatic. Sometimes it's just listening well, offering a prayer, helping with a practical need, or sharing honestly how Jesus has changed me. What matters is that His life in me keeps flowing outward instead of stopping with me. The invitation is simply to stay close to Him and trust that His life will reach others through mine.

Luke 19:10 —For the Son of Man came to seek and save the lost. **Galatians 3:8** — And the Scripture, foreseeing that God would justify the

Gentiles by faith, preached the Gospel beforehand to Abraham, saying, "In you shall all the nations be blessed." **Matthew 28:18–20** – And Jesus came and said to them, "All authority in heaven and on earth has been given to me. Go therefore and make disciples of all nations, baptizing them in the name of the Father and of the Son and of the Holy Spirit, teaching them to observe all that I have commanded you. And behold, I am with you always, to the end of the age." **Acts 1:8** – But you will receive power when the Holy Spirit has come upon you, and you will be my witnesses in Jerusalem and in all Judea and Samaria, and to the end of the earth. **2 Corinthians 5:17–20** – Therefore, if anyone is in Christ, he is a new creation. The old has passed away; behold, the new has come. All this is from God, who through Christ reconciled us to himself and gave us the ministry of reconciliation; that is, in Christ God was reconciling the world to himself, not counting their trespasses against them, and entrusting to us the message of reconciliation. Therefore, we are ambassadors for Christ, God making his appeal through us. We implore you on behalf of Christ, be reconciled to God.

42. Home at last: abiding now, and the hope of glory

The abiding life is both a present reality and a foretaste of future glory. Even now, Christ in me is "the hope of glory," giving me daily access to the God I will one day see face to face. His indwelling presence means that, in the deepest sense, I am already at home in

Him, even as I still walk as a pilgrim through a broken world. Yet a day is coming when faith will give way to sight, when the branches will share the Vine's life with no more sin, sorrow, or hindrance to joy. All that now dims my awareness of His nearness—fear, distraction, and the pull of sin—will be taken away, and the Life that has sustained me from within will be the light that fills everything. **In the renewed creation, the God who has made His home in me will bring me fully into His home, and the homesickness I have carried all my days will finally be healed.** Until then, I abide with Him here, learning to receive both joy and sorrow as part of the journey toward that day. Each act of trust, each quiet surrender, becomes a small rehearsal for the life to come, when the people of God will be gathered as one and abiding will be no longer resisted but enjoyed in unhindered, face-to-face communion with the One who has always held me fast. The home I am moving toward is not a courtroom where my case is closed, but a feast where the Vine and His branches rejoice together forever.

Colossians 1:27 – To them God chose to make known how great among the Gentiles are the riches of the glory of this mystery, which is Christ in you, the hope of glory. **John 14:2–3** – In my Father's house are many rooms. If it were not so, would I have told you that I go to prepare a place for you? And if I go and prepare a place for you, I will come again and will take you to myself, that where I am you may be also. **Revelation 21:1–4** Then I saw a new heaven and a new earth, for the first heaven and the first earth had passed away, and the sea was no more. And I saw the holy city, new Jerusalem, coming down out of heaven from God, prepared as a bride adorned for her husband. And I heard a loud voice from the throne saying, "Behold, the dwelling place of God is with man. He will dwell with them, and they will be his people, and God himself will be with them as their God. He will wipe away every tear from their eyes, and death shall be no more, neither shall there be mourning, nor crying, nor pain anymore, for the former things have passed away." **1 Thessalonians 4:16–18** – For the Lord himself will descend from heaven with a cry of command, with the voice of an archangel, and with the sound of the trumpet of God. And the dead in Christ will rise first. Then we who are alive, who are left, will be caught up together with them in the clouds to meet the Lord in the air, and so we will always be with the Lord. Therefore, encourage one another with these words.

Thoughts & Observations

The Abiding Life

One-Sentence Summaries for meditation and reflection

1. My heart carries a deep, often unnamed ache for home that no earthly place can fully satisfy.
2. In Christ, God has made His home in my heart so that I am no longer a spiritual orphan but His beloved dwelling.
3. Jesus invites me to make my home in Him, living in conscious, trusting fellowship with the One who already lives in me.
4. Jesus is the true Vine and I am a branch, created not to live for Him in my own strength but to live from His life flowing through me.
5. My Father is the wise Vinedresser who lovingly tends and prunes my life for lasting fruit, not punishment.
6. I have already been cleansed and decisively "pruned" by His Word, so further

pruning is never about earning acceptance but about more life.

7. The Father continues to prune me, removing even good things at times, so that a deeper, quieter fruitfulness can ripen in me.

8. Abiding means the very life of Jesus—His compassion, purity, and strength—flows through me like sap through a branch, producing fruit I could never manufacture.

9. The fruit God seeks is Jesus' own character reproduced in me by the Spirit, not my impressiveness or performance.

10. Apart from Jesus I can do nothing of eternal value, but dependence on Him opens my life to His abundance and power.

11. Abiding in His Word means letting Jesus' words live in me until His truth becomes the atmosphere my mind and heart breathe so I might experience His freedom and joy.

12. Jesus calls me to remain in the circle of His love, and His commands show me

how to walk in that love rather than earn it.

13. Obedience does not secure God's love; it is how I abide in and enjoy the love that is already mine in Christ.

14. As I taste more of Christ's love, I live as a homesick pilgrim who is already at home in Him, awaiting the day I see Him face to face.

15. Jesus' teaching on abiding finds its deep echo in Paul's language of *me in Christ and Christ in me*. In the first incarnation, the eternal Son took on flesh—He lived, died, and rose in my place so that my standing with God rests entirely on His work not mine.

16. Flowing from that, the "second incarnation" means this same Christ now lives within me by His Spirit and unites me to Himself, so that my real humanity becomes His temple and my life is hidden with Him in God.

17. The normal Christian life is not occasional experiences with God but a daily, grace-given walk with Christ who is always with me and for me.

18. Jesus frees me from outside-in religion by giving me an inside-out life where change flows from His indwelling presence, not my self-improvement.

19. My old self was crucified with Christ so that I am no longer defined or ruled by who I used to be.

20. Because I have been crucified with Christ, the life I now live is no longer "I, trying harder," but Christ living in me as I trust Him.

21. Walking by the Spirit means Jesus Himself lives through me, empowering me to do what I could never do by willpower alone.

22. Christ gave Himself for my sins to rescue me from this present evil age, not just to give me heaven later but to free me from its enslaving patterns now.

23. In Christ there is no condemnation; the treadmill of guilt and performance is broken, and I stand on the solid ground of His righteousness.

24. Grace is not just the way I begin the Christian life; it is the ongoing engine of

change that trains me to say no to sin and yes to a life that reflects Jesus.

25. Christ lives in me as a settled reality, and over time His life presses outward so that I begin to look, think, feel, and act more like Him.
26. Spiritual formation is not my self-help project but the Spirit's lifelong artistry, using every season to conform me to Christ as I keep presenting myself to God.
27. Christ has set me free not to indulge my flesh but to love and serve others in the power of His indwelling life.
28. Love is the fulfillment of the law as Christ lives His love through me toward others in concrete, Spirit-enabled ways.
29. The fruit of the Spirit is Jesus' life made visible in my attitudes and reactions, so that people taste something of Him when they encounter me.
30. In my relationships, Jesus lives through me, teaching me to love, forgive, listen, and serve as a branch sharing His life.

31. In failure and weakness, Jesus meets me not with rejection but with grace, turning my inadequacy into a place where His strength is displayed.

32. In opportunities and risks, Jesus living through me enables courage, generosity, and obedience that are beyond my natural resources.

33. In the mundane and monotonous, Christ's indwelling presence dignifies ordinary moments and turns daily routines into places of quiet communion.

34. The Spirit is leading me from God-amnesia to God-awareness, learning to notice and respond to Jesus' presence in the flow of my day.

35. In silent prayer, I rest in the One who lives in me, letting go of striving so that my heart can simply be with Him.

36. Through slow, Spirit-guided Scripture, I abide in His Word, allowing His truth to renew my mind and shape my desires.

37. My simple daily confession—"Jesus, You live in me; live Your life through me today, for the sake of others"—

reorients my day around His indwelling life and mission.

38. Trials and pruning are the Father's wise love at work, not to harm me but to deepen my trust and make me more fruitful in Christ.

39. Abiding is never just "Christ in me" but "Christ in us," as we share His life together as His body.

40. Because Jesus lives in me, every day and place becomes part of His ongoing mission as He loves and serves others through me.

41. I live as a branch on mission now, knowing that one day the story will end with me fully at home with Him in glory.

42. Abiding now in Christ is a foretaste of the day when my homesickness will be healed forever and I will dwell with Him in the fullness of His kingdom.

Now, if you're wondering, "What does all this actually look like in my daily life?" turn the page. The five "Practicing the Abiding Life" guides that follow are meant to help you continue to learn, with others, how to live the abiding life.

Part IV

Practicing
The Abiding Life:
Guides for the Journey

The Practice of Silence and Solitude

In John 15, Jesus invites us into the most intimate reality of the Christian life: "Abide in me, and I in you" (v. 4). This abiding isn't a background hum we can maintain amid constant noise and hurry. The branch draws life from the Vine only when it remains attached—unhurried, undistracted, open to the flow of sap. Solitude and silence are the quiet garden where we intentionally position ourselves to stay connected. Without them, we risk living as branches that look alive on the outside but slowly wither because we're too busy to receive the life Christ longs to pour into us. In the noise of our world, solitude becomes an act of faith: we step away not to escape life, but to let the true Life enter more fully.

Silence is where abiding deepens. Jesus often withdrew to solitary places to pray (Luke 5:16), modeling for us the need to quiet our inner chatter so we can hear His voice. In John 15, He says, "If you abide in me, and my words abide in you …" (v. 7). His words don't take root in a soul cluttered with competing voices—social media, worries, self-talk, endless to-do lists. Silence creates space for Scripture to sink in, for the Spirit to speak, for the Father's pruning hand to be felt without resistance. In silence, we stop performing and start receiving; we let go of our frantic attempts to produce fruit and allow Christ to live His fruitful life through us.

This practice isn't about earning God's favor or proving our spirituality. It's about protection and preparation. Just as the vinedresser prunes the fruitful branch to make it even more fruitful (John 15:2), solitude and silence expose what's merely leafy busyness so the Father can lovingly cut it away. In the quiet, illusions of self-sufficiency fade, distractions lose their grip, and we rediscover our dependence on Jesus. What feels like emptiness at first becomes fertile soil where the life of the Vine can grow deeper roots. The slow, hidden work in silence often yields the richest fruit later—love, joy, peace, patience—that shows up in our relationships and daily choices.

Ultimately, solitude and silence are invitations to rest in the One who already abides in us. Jesus doesn't call us to strive for connection; He calls us to remain in the connection that's already ours. In the stillness, we taste the truth of "Christ in me" more vividly. We hear His gentle "remain," feel His life flowing, and emerge not drained, but renewed—ready to bear fruit that lasts because it comes not from us, but from Him. Make space for these quiet moments. They are not luxuries; they are lifelines to the Vine.[2]

---

[2] For more on "*The Abiding Life,*" see my message at: https://www.fellowshipgreenville.org/message/the-abiding-life

Spirit-Guided, Gospel-Meditation

"Spirit-Guided, Gospel-Meditation" is a way to read the Bible in a slow, prayerful, and reflective way, in keeping with the invitation to mediate on Scripture from Psalm 1 which I believe aligns with Jesus' invitation to "Abide in My word." It is not a rigid formula but a gentle rhythm you can adapt to your own pace and personality. The goal is not to "get through" Scripture quickly, but to let Scripture get through to you—until the Word that you read, begins to read you, forming Christ in you.

Three Simple Movements

1. **Pause and Pray** – Begin by slowing down. Take 2–3 slow, deep breaths to quiet your mind and body. Become present to the presence of God who is already with you and in you. Pray a simple opening prayer: "Holy Spirit, take God's Word in this text and make it God's Word to me today." or "Come, Holy Spirit. I am listening. Open my eyes to see and my ears to hear what You want to say to me in this passage."

The aim is not to empty your mind, but to fill it with expectancy that Jesus Himself will meet you in His Word.

2. **Read, Reflect, Write** – Choose a small portion of Scripture from one of the Gospels—5–10 verses, often a single scene or teaching of Jesus.

   Read slowly – 2–3 times, perhaps aloud or under your breath. Savor the words like food.

   Reflect – Step imaginatively into the scene. Picture Jesus speaking these words to you personally. Let the Word read you as you read it. Ask gentle, open questions:

   - What word, phrase, or image stands out or tugs at my heart?
   - What do I feel as I sit with it—comfort, conviction, invitation, resistance?
   - What is Jesus revealing about Himself here?
   - What might the Spirit be inviting me into today?

- How does this truth read me—expose my fears, pride, unbelief, or longing?

  Write – Put into simple words what you sense God saying. No need for eloquence; a journal sentence or two is enough. Example: "Jesus, because You are God's beloved Son who died and rose for me, I too am God's beloved child. Thank You. Help me rest in that today."

3. **Pray and Pass It On** – Pray back what you've heard: "Jesus, You live in me. Live Your life through me today—for the sake of others." Ask the Spirit to press the truth deeper and to bring it to mind during the day. Then release it: "Lord, if someone in my path today needs encouragement from what You've shown me in Your Word today, prompt me to share it with them in a personal, conversational way."

Over time, you may find the same truth returning in conversations, decisions, or trials—evidence that the Word is taking root, so that your daily confession, "Jesus, You live in me; live Your life through me, today for the sake of others," becomes far more than words: it becomes the quiet, steady rhythm of your day.

A Few Encouragements

- Your mind will wander. That's normal. Gently return it to Jesus without self-criticism.
- Some mornings feel rich; others feel dry. Faithfulness matters more than feelings.
- Start small—5 minutes is enough to begin.
- The Gospels are especially fruitful for this practice because they let you walk with Jesus moment by moment.

May this rhythm become a daily homecoming—returning to the stream of God's Word until your life grows like a tree planted by living water, yielding fruit in season for His glory and others' good.[3]

---

[3] If you would like to dig deeper into *"Spirit-Guided, Gospel Meditation"* see my message at: https://www.fellowshipgreenville.org/message/spirit-guided-Gospel-meditation. Also, check out the study notes and additional resource pdfs by Dallas Willard and others as well.

Experiencing Freedom through Abiding in the Word

"If you abide in my word, you truly are my disciples, and you will know the truth, and the truth will set you free." (John 8:31–32)

My growing conviction is that Jesus' invitation to "abide in My word" is first and foremost a freedom invitation. He is not handing out another religious task or a heavier spiritual to-do list. He is opening a door into a way of life where His Word becomes the atmosphere I breathe, the story I live in, and the truth that actually sets me free. The promise is that I will come to know the truth—know it in an experiential, lived way—and enjoy the freedom Jesus won for me on the Cross.

I have believed this promise for years in a general sense, but I am coming to see how specific and concrete Jesus intends it to be. When I honestly look at my life, I can name places where I have not lived free: the pull to perform, the need to look good in other people's eyes, the frantic replanning when I can't control outcomes, the noisy loop of self-criticism that runs in my head. The unsettling question Jesus presses on me is this: in these places, am I really taking Him at His Word?

As I've sat with John 8, I've become more aware of the fleshly patterns I embraced growing up in a fallen, broken world and that continue to dog me still—carefully managed public faces that I want others to see. These "personas" are often built on self-deception. They are the faces I put on to appear competent, in control, spiritual, impressive. Alongside them are the preoccupations that enslave me: the mental conversations I rehearse, the imagined criticisms, the internal courtroom where I'm continually on trial. These thoughts run like a fixed loop in my mind.

Abiding in Jesus' Word confronts these fleshly patterns. His Word tells me who I really am in Him: a beloved child, deeply known, fully forgiven, delighted in. His Word also exposes the ways I grasp for worth apart from him. When I choose to live from these patterns instead of from my identity in Christ, I step out of the freedom He offers and back into slavery—slavery to sin, to fear, to the opinions of others. Abiding in His Word is how the Spirit keeps exposing those old flesh-patterns and training me to live from who I already am in Christ.

Jesus' promise in John 8 begins with a small but weighty word: "*If*." "*If* you abide in My word, you truly are my disciples." That little word tells me it is possible to believe many right things about Jesus and yet not live as His disciple. The Jews in John 8 are described as those who had believed Him, and yet as the chapter unfolds, their refusal to receive His Word exposes that they are not free and still slaves to sin.

This pushes me to ask uncomfortable questions. In what areas do I say I believe Jesus but refuse to let His Word define reality for me? Where am I holding on to my own interpretations, my own judgments, my own plans, instead of submitting them to what He says?

Abiding is not merely reading His words or agreeing with them in theory; it is remaining in them, living in them, letting them be the truest thing about everything because, ultimately, He is the *Living* Word that lives in me.

When Jesus promises that I will "know the truth," He is not talking about abstract, theoretical knowledge. He is inviting me into a kind of "knowing" that is tested and proven in the actual pressures of life. I know the truth about His forgiveness when I bring my real sin into the light and experience His cleansing. I know the truth about His presence when I walk through fear and discover that I am not alone. I know the truth about His care when I entrust Him with outcomes that I cannot control and find that I am held.

This means that abiding in His Word is deeply connected to my lived experience. Scripture is not meant to hover above my life as a detached set of doctrines. It is meant to sink into my daily life—into conflicts, disappointments, criticism, illness, financial uncertainty, relational pain. As I meet Him there, His Word moves from being something I merely affirm to something I actually rely on.

One situation that has exposed my lack of abiding is unresolved conflict. I find myself replaying conversations, defending myself in my mind, crafting better responses I wish I had said. I imagine what the other person thinks of me. I try to figure out how to fix things or manage their perception. All of this feels active and responsible, but in truth it is often a way of leaning on my own understanding.

In those moments, Jesus invites me to abide in His Word. His Word tells me that He is the one who justifies; that He sees and knows the truth; that He is with me when I am misunderstood; that I am, in Him, already fully accepted by the Father. When I take those words seriously—when I choose to trust them more than I trust the story in my head—I begin to experience freedom. The loop quietens. The need to defend myself loses some of its grip. I can move toward the other person in humility and love instead of fear and control. This is what it looks like, in a very ordinary situation, to know the truth and live free in Christ.

If my mind is going to live in this kind of truth, it has to be renewed and re-trained. My default is to let the day's events, other people's opinions, and my own inner narrator set the tone. Abiding in Jesus' Word means my mind and heart must be schooled in a different way. I need a steady, daily re-directing of my attention back to the Gospel stories.

Practically, this means taking a particular scene from the Gospels and living with it, not just reading it once and moving on. I read and re-read it. I picture it. I imagine the sights, sounds, and expressions. I pay attention to how Jesus moves toward people, how He responds to pressure, how He rests in His Father's love. I carry that scene with me into the day. As situations arise, I ask, "What would it look like to respond here out of the same confidence and dependence I see in Jesus?" In this way, I am not merely learning *about* Him; I am walking *with* Him, living *from* Him moment by moment.

One of the striking things about John 8 is how Jesus navigates harsh opposition. He is questioned, accused, misunderstood, and openly resisted. Yet He is not thrown off balance. He speaks from a different level, a top-down perspective. He lives and reasons from what He has seen with the Father and what He has heard from the Father—"You are my beloved Son, in whom I am well-pleased." His words and responses are anchored in that reality rather than in the swirl of what people around him are saying and doing.

Abiding in His Word invites me into that same top-down way of seeing. When I face criticism, uncertainty, or pressure, my instincts are all bottom-up: I read the situation primarily through my emotions, my fears, and others' reactions. Jesus calls me instead to start with what the Father has already said in His word: who God is, who I am in Christ, what is ultimately true about the future. As I let those truths frame the moment, I find that I am less captive to what is loud and immediate. I can respond more like a son who trusts his Father than like an orphan scrambling to protect himself.

Sitting with this chapter has shown me that my thoughts will not remain neutral. Either I take them captive to the word of Christ, or they will take me captive. When I meditate on my fears, my grievances, my imagined scenarios, they shape me. They bend my heart away from trust and toward self-reliance. They convince me that I must manage my life on my own.

Abiding in Jesus' Word is the Spirit-empowered practice of interrupting that process. It is noticing when my mind has slipped into old patterns and choosing to return to what he has said. Sometimes that means speaking His Word out loud. Sometimes it means praying it back to Him. Sometimes it means simply sitting in silence and letting a single phrase settle into me: "You are my beloved child," "I am with you," "My grace is sufficient for you." Over time, this returning becomes a habit—a new default setting for my heart.

One of the most precious freedoms Jesus has been offering me through this abiding is freedom from pretense and performance. I feel a deep, persistent pull to show up as the version of myself that looks most impressive, most put together, most spiritually mature. Even my engagement with Scripture can become another arena for that performance: I want to "have something good to say," to sound insightful, to appear wise.

But when I meet Him in His Word as I really am—weak, distracted, fearful, hungry—something shifts. His Word reminds me that He did not choose me because I am impressive. It invites me to drop the act and come as a beloved child who is already fully known. In that place, I can listen instead of perform; I can receive instead of manage; I can confess instead of conceal. This is a different kind of life, and it is the life His Word is always offering me.

As this chapter of John continues, the contrast sharpens between those who cling to their own understanding and those who receive Jesus' word as truth. I hear His questions as if they were directed to me: "Why do you not understand what I say? It is because you cannot bear to hear my word" (John 8:43). I don't want that to be true of me. I want to be the kind of person who can bear His word and hear His word – who welcomes it, submits to it, and finds life in it.

So, my response becomes a prayer:

"Lord Jesus, teach me to abide in Your Word. Protect me from fleshly patterns, from the places I hide, and from the preoccupations that enslave my mind. Show me where I am not taking You at Your Word, where I still lean on my own understanding. Train my heart to live from the story of Your life—to see my world from the Father's perspective and to rest in Your love. Father, Son, and Spirit, give me grace to trust You with all my heart and to rest in Your sovereign care. Let Your Word be the truth I not only affirm but actually live, so that I might truly be Your disciple and slowly experience the freedom You so gladly give, just as You promised:

If the Son sets you free, you will be free indeed.
(John 8:36)

Fruit-bearing vs Achieving

Fruit is one of Jesus' favorite ways to talk about the Christian life. In John 15, on the night before His crucifixion, He does not send His friends out to achieve great things for God. He invites them into something far more intimate: "Abide in Me." The picture He gives them is tender and relational. He is the true vine. His Father is the vinedresser. We are the branches. Our primary calling is not to perform for Him or to produce for Him, but to simply dwell with Him.

If you read John 15 slowly, you can almost feel Jesus repeating Himself on purpose. He talks about fruit, more fruit, much fruit, and fruit that remains. He is pressing a simple truth into the hearts of His disciples: the Father is glorified, not when they become impressive in the world's eyes, but when their lives quietly bear His kind of fruit. In other words, God is not asking for a heroic performance. He is asking for a deep, steady, daily abiding.

That is good news for weary strivers. So many of us live with a low-grade pressure humming in the background of our souls: "Have I done enough? Am I where I should be by now? Do I have anything to show for my life?" We look around, we compare, and we feel the ache of not measuring up. The world disciples us to think in terms of achievement: what have you produced, built, collected, or accomplished that others would admire?

Achievement is not always bad. Many of our accomplishments are good gifts. Earning a degree, doing our work well, providing for a family, leading a ministry, writing a book, building something that serves people—these can be beautiful acts of stewardship. But there is a subtle shift that can happen inside. Without noticing it, we begin to rest the weight of our identity on what we have done rather than on who we are in Christ. Our sense of value rises and falls with our performance.

Jesus, in John 15, gently cuts through all of that. He takes the conversation out of the world of scorecards and into the world of vineyards. Branches do not stress about their résumé. They are not trying to outproduce the branch next to them. They simply stay connected to the vine. The fruit comes, not because the branch is impressive, but because the life of the vine is moving through it.

That is what fruitfulness is: the life of Christ flowing into us and then out of us in ways that bless others. Fruit is His character slowly taking shape in our hearts—love, joy, peace, patience, kindness, goodness, faithfulness, gentleness, self-control. Fruit is the quiet endurance that keeps showing up when it would be easier to quit. Fruit is the courage to repent, to forgive, to ask forgiveness, to keep walking in the light. Fruit is the good works that no one sees but the Father—the prayers whispered for others, the acts of mercy done in secret, the listening ear given to someone who is hurting.

In that sense, fruit is always for others. No one plants a tree so the fruit can admire itself. Fruit is meant to be tasted, shared, received. Spiritual fruit is like that. It nourishes the people around us. It brings a little more of God's comfort, wisdom, and presence into their ordinary days. And here is the mystery: much of this fruit will never make a headline, never trend, never be counted on a spreadsheet. But heaven notices. The Father is glorified.

This means a life can look very "small" on paper and yet be overflowing with fruit. Think of the faithful believer who quietly loves their family, serves in their church, works with integrity, and keeps a soft heart toward God over the long haul. Think of the person who prays, encourages, and shows up for people in crisis, who carries others' burdens in prayer and friendship. That may not look like much to the watching world, but in the kingdom, this is beautiful fruit.

Jesus' own life shows us this so clearly. If we judged His life by the world's standards of success, it would look almost like a failure. He spent thirty years in obscurity. His public ministry was short. He never wrote a book, never held an office, never commanded an army. At the end, He was rejected, mocked, and crucified. Yet no life has ever been more fruitful. Through His life, death, and resurrection He opened the way to the Father, defeated sin and death, and brought forth a people who will be His forever. His story tells us plainly: you do not have to be "successful" in the eyes of the world to be deeply fruitful in the eyes of God.

This is why the Father's pruning is actually a gift, even when it doesn't feel like it. Jesus says that every branch that does bear fruit the Father prunes so that it will bear more fruit. Pruning can look like closed doors, disappointments, limitations, or losses that we did not want. It can look like the Lord quietly removing things we were using to prop up our identity—roles, recognition, achievements, or plans that had become too central in our hearts.

In those seasons, it is easy to feel like we are going backward. But pruning is never punishment for a branch that is abiding; it is preparation for deeper fruitfulness. The Father knows what weakens us, what distracts us, what feeds our addiction to achievement. In love, He cuts those things away so that more of His Son's life can flow freely in us. Often, the seasons that feel least "productive" on the surface are the ones where God is doing His deepest work in our souls.

So the question slowly changes. Instead of endlessly asking, "What am I accomplishing?" we begin to ask, "Am I abiding?" Am I choosing to create space in my day to enjoy His presence with me? Am I letting His words remain in me? Am I learning to trust His heart, even when I do not see what He is doing? Am I letting Him define what fruitfulness looks like in this season of my life?

As that question takes root, something gentle happens inside. Pressure gives way to peace.

The tightness in the chest starts to loosen. The constant inner critic quiets down. The need to compare our story to someone else's begins to fade. We become more grateful for the small, ordinary ways God is present with us. We begin to see that the real miracle is not that we do great things for God, but that God—by grace—would choose to live His life in and through us at all.

If you belong to Christ, you are already a branch in His vine. You do not have to earn your way into that place; you are there by grace. The Father is not standing over you with a clipboard, checking whether you are impressive enough. He is a wise and loving vinedresser, patiently tending your life and inviting you more deeply into His Son.

So hear again the simple, life-giving invitation of Jesus: "*Abide in Me.*" Bring Him your fears, your failures, your hopes, your exhaustion. Let His word wash over you. Let His love settle on you. Let His Spirit nudge you toward small, concrete steps of faithfulness. Over time, you will look back and discover that, almost without realizing it, He has been bearing fruit through your life—fruit that blesses others, glorifies the Father, and remains.

Joy is the Music of Abiding

"These things I have spoken to you, that my joy may be in you, and that your joy may be full."
(John 15:11).

When Jesus talks about abiding, He does not just talk about pruning, dependence, and fruit; He also talks about joy. "These things I have spoken to you," He says, "that My joy may be in you, and that your joy may be full." The same Lord who tells me, "Apart from Me you can do nothing," speaks these words so that His own joy might live in me. Joy is not a perk reserved for unusually upbeat Christians; it is part of the normal abiding life He describes when He calls me to abide in Him, in His Word, and in His love.

As an older man, possibly in his 90's, the apostle John had lived the abiding life for a lifetime. The young disciple who leaned on Jesus' chest in the upper room became the elderly pastor in Ephesus, still talking about fellowship with the Father and the Son, still speaking about love, truth, and joy. When he writes his letters near the end of his life, you can hear John 15 still echoing in his heart. He is no longer just recording Jesus' words about joy and abiding; he is bearing witness to how joy and abiding fit together over decades.

Jesus roots this joy in love. "As the Father has loved Me, so have I loved you. Abide in My love…These things I have spoken to you, that My joy may be in you, and that your joy may be full" (John 15:9, 11). As I begin to trust that "as the Father has loved Me, so have I loved you," I no longer stand outside, hoping to be allowed in. By grace, I am already inside the circle of love, welcomed and secure. Obedience then becomes the way I remain within the warmth of that love, not the price I pay to earn it. Years later John will say that his purpose in writing is that his readers would share in this fellowship with the Father and the Son—and that in this shared life "our joy may be complete." He is simply unpacking what Jesus promised that last night: that real joy grows where abiding fellowship is real.

In a very real sense, "*Joy is the music of the abiding life*." Music is what happens when notes, timing, and tone come together in a way that reflects the composer's heart. Joy is what happens when the truths of the Gospel, the presence of Christ in me, and the Father's wise pruning all come together in a life being tuned to His heart. Joy often begins as relief—

the treadmill of performance slows and finally stops. Over time, that relief ripens into gratitude, and gratitude ripens into joy. The Spirit causes "love, joy, peace..." to grow as the fruit of Christ's indwelling life, not as the result of my religious willpower. Joy is the inner music the Spirit plays beneath the noise of my days—sometimes loud and unmistakable, sometimes a quiet, steady note that keeps me from despair—but always a gift.

Of course, pruning does not feel joyful. The Father's cuts can look like loss, delay, or limitation. Yet the same Scriptures that speak of trials and discipline also invite me to "count it all joy" when I meet various trials and promise that the Father's loving discipline "later yields the peaceful fruit of righteousness." Pruning is not payback but preparation for more life. Joy in pruning does not mean I enjoy the pain; it means that, beneath the pain, I am learning to say, "My Father is here. He is wise. He is after more of Jesus' life being expressed in and through me." When I remember that I am "already clean" because of the word Jesus has spoken, I can begin to receive even painful seasons as the careful pruning of a Vinedresser who is more committed to my fruitfulness than I am.

If pruning tests joy in my circumstances, weakness tests joy in my own heart. I might expect joy only in my victories, but the Gospel teaches me to find it even in weakness. John invites me to "walk in the light" as God is in the light, and there to know both cleansing and fellowship. To walk in the light is to bring my sins, worries, inadequacies, fears—everything—into the presence of God, and often into the presence of trusted brothers and sisters. In those honest, light-filled places, a surprising joy appears. It is not joy in my sin, but joy in a fresh experience of forgiving grace; joy in an Advocate who keeps interceding; joy in the slow but real evidence that my failures no longer get the last word. My weakness becomes a stage on which Christ's strength can be displayed. John can write so that "our joy may be complete" because he knows that joy grows in lives where the light is winning new territory and where the love of Christ, not the shame of the past, has the final say.

Most days, though, joy is lived in the ordinary. The abiding life unfolds in quiet routines and unseen acts of love—in kitchens and cubicles, car lines and care facilities, emails and errands and unremarkable

Tuesdays. When I remember that Jesus is actually living through me in the ordinary—through a kind word to a coworker, a patient response to a child, a listening ear for a friend—then the smallest acts of love become holy ground. Joy comes as I realize that I am not just "getting through" a day; I am sharing a day with the One who lives in me.

Listen again to older John's voice: "I rejoiced greatly to find some of your children walking in the truth," and, "I have no greater joy than to hear that my children are walking in the truth" (3 John 3,4). His deepest joy, after a lifetime of abiding, is to see others live their daily lives in the reality of Jesus. That same joy is offered to every parent, grandparent, and disciple-maker who watches the next generation learn to abide—children and spiritual children "walking in the truth," moving through their days with Jesus living in them and through them.

All these small flashes of joy in ordinary days are not random; they are previews of where the story is headed. From the beginning of this primer, I have spoken of homesickness—the ache for a better country, a truer home. That ache remains until the day I see Jesus, but the God who will one day welcome me home has already made His home in me. Christ in me is "the hope of glory," and every glimpse of His joy now is a small taste of the joy that will one day fill everything. John encourages me to "abide in Him, so that when He appears we may have confidence and not shrink from Him in shame at His coming." That future day will be the moment when the music of joy, which now plays under the noise of a broken world, is turned up to full volume. There will be no more painful pruning, no more wrestling with the flesh, no more tears of regret—only the fullness of joy in the presence of the One who has been living in me all along.

Until then, joyful abiding is not an assignment to complete but a life to receive. Jesus does not command me to manufacture joy for Him; He invites me to remain in Him so that His joy may be in me. My part is to rest in His presence, listening for the music of His joy, trusting it, and slowly learning to sing along.

Conclusion

Until Christ Is Formed in You

As we come to the end of our *Abiding Life* journey, one prayer keeps rising in my heart—the same prayer Paul carried for the Galatians: "my little children, for whom I am again in the anguish of childbirth until Christ is formed in you!" (Galatians 4:19). That is my longing for you, and for myself, as we step into whatever days lie ahead: not that we would simply know more about Jesus, or try harder to imitate Him from the outside-in, but that Christ Himself would be more fully formed in us—His love, His joy, His patience, His forgiveness, His courage—taking visible shape in our attitudes, reactions, words, and relationships.

Day by day, in the very real contours of your story, may the Spirit take what is true of you in Christ and make it more deeply real to your heart, your habits, your relationships, and your life together with His people. This is the normal Christian life—Christ within you, quietly forming His life in you by His grace.

Again, remember that Paul spoke those words to a whole church; in the same way, my longing is not only that Christ be formed in you personally, but that He be formed among us together, so that our shared life as His body looks more like Jesus.

So, let me ask you the same question I've been asking myself. Looking back over the past year, is my life reflecting more of Jesus' love, joy, patience, forgiveness, and grace? Or turned the other way—am I becoming less anxious, less angry, less selfish, less envious, less resentful?

Hear me: I am not asking these questions to heap guilt on you or to drive you into another cycle of "try-harder-to-do-better" religion, but simply to stir an honest reflection of desire. If we truly want to grow more conformed to the image of Christ going forward, how do we partner with God in that process?

You have walked through this Primer not to learn a new technique, but to pay attention to a reality that was true the moment you trusted Jesus: He lives in you, and you live in Him. The Father has made His home in your heart, the Son shares His own life with you, and the Spirit quietly works in all things to form Christ in you for the glory of God and the good of others.

Nothing in these pages has asked you to add one more burden to an already crowded life. Instead, the invitation has been to lay down the burden of self-salvation and self-transformation, and to entrust yourself again and again to the Vine who supplies everything a branch needs. Your part is not to manufacture holiness, fruit, or impact; your part is to remain in the One who has already bound Himself to you in covenant love, letting His grace, His Word, and His Spirit do what you cannot do for yourself.

This abiding life will move through "seasons" you would not have chosen—pruning and weakness, waiting and everyday days that feel small and unseen. Yet in all of it, the Father is tending you with the same wise love with which He tended His firstborn Son, using every joy and sorrow as material for Christ to be formed in you. This is the way of Psalm 1: like a tree planted by streams of water, which yields its fruit *in season* and whose leaf does not wither, even when the weather turns harsh.

All along the way, Jesus walks with you and lives in you, meeting you in everyday life and in weakness, teaching you to trust His love, receive His grace, and share His life with others. He is the One who planted this deep homesickness in your heart, and He is the One who quietly satisfies it even now as He makes His home in you. And one day, when faith becomes sight, the homesickness that has followed you through every season will be healed at last as you see Him face to face, finally at home with Him.

The more you yield to this work of grace, the more your ordinary story becomes a place where others can taste something of Jesus—His patience in your irritations, His mercy in your failures, His courage in your risks, His hope in your sufferings. One day, the homesickness that has hummed beneath your life will finally be answered: the Christ who now lives in you will stand before you, and the God who made His home in your heart will welcome you fully into His home, where the Vine and the branches will share unhindered joy forever. Until that day, you walk by faith and not by sight, trusting that "Christ in you" really is "the hope of glory," and that no act of hidden faithfulness, no quiet yes to His indwelling life, is ever wasted.

So tomorrow, as you step back into your real life—your people, your work, your limits, your story—may this simple confession become the quiet rhythm of your days:

Jesus, You live in me; live Your life through me, for the sake of others.

And may "the God of peace…equip you with everything good that you may do His will, working in you that which is pleasing in His sight, through Jesus Christ, to whom be glory forever and ever. Amen." (Hebrews 13:20–21)

Grace and peace to you in the abiding life of Jesus, until the day we are finally at home with Him.

Abide in Me,
Abide in My Love,
Abide in My Word,
and you will bear much fruit.
These things I have spoken to you,
that My joy may be in you
and that
your joy may be full.

Acknowledgments

This *Primer on the Abiding Life* has been shaped by the faithful community God has placed around me.

It began with my wife, Karen. From the first whisper of this idea, she has been my cheerleader. Her steadfast love and encouragement made space for this project to be born, and her belief in me never wavered.

When I finally had a rough draft, I shared it with my friend and Executive Pastor, Rob Marks. His response brought tears to my eyes. He said, "We have to get this to our people." In that moment, his enthusiasm gave me the courage to believe this message might truly help others.

I am deeply thankful for Raydell Tedder and Carolyn Kennedy. They both spent countless hours walking through multiple versions of the manuscript with patience and care. Beyond catching errors, they helped me say what I wanted to say more clearly. They asked thoughtful questions and offered wise counsel, and this Primer is better because of their labor.

Steven Halbert skillfully guided me through the Amazon KDP process. I am sincerely grateful for his help.

Dr. Gene Getz—pastor, professor, and author—whose philosophy of "fellowship-style" church ministry has profoundly shaped my own, offered invaluable feedback that helped me more clearly see and articulate the corporate and communal dimensions of abiding in Christ. For this, I am deeply thankful for his contribution to this Primer.

I also want to thank my friend Chuck Gschwend and the folks at The Eden Project for helping me find my own "journey home" in the abiding life in Christ. Their influence runs deeper than these pages can express.

And to the community of Fellowship Greenville—my church family for the past thirty years: you have walked with me, shaped me, and graciously listened as many of these ideas were first preached from the pulpit. This book grew up among you, and I remain deeply grateful for you.

Charlie Boyd is a veteran pastor-teacher who has served the body of Christ for more than forty-five years, the last three decades at Fellowship Greenville in South Carolina. His preaching is expositional and gospel-centered, marked by a "big idea" narrative style shaped by doctoral work in preaching and homiletics. He loves helping people see how the story of Scripture reshapes everyday life in Christ as well as mentoring younger preachers in clear, text-driven, Christ-centered exposition. *The Abiding Life Primer* grew out of a season of preaching and personal reflection on what it means to abide in Jesus – truths first lived and taught among the people of Fellowship Greenville. Charlie graduated from Dallas Theological Seminary (Th.M.) and Gordon-Conwell Theological Seminary (D.Min.). He and his wife, Karen, have been married for forty-nine years and have three children and nine grandchildren. His deepest desire is to help people move from a "try-harder-do-better" religion into a day-by-day, grace-dependent relationship with the indwelling Christ.

Other works:

Different Children Different Needs – a parenting resource

What God Has Always Wanted – a children's bible story book

www.ingramcontent.com/pod-product-compliance
Lightning Source LLC
LaVergne TN
LVHW090526110826
845146LV00003B/999

9798995489108